Helion & Company Limited
Unit 8 Amherst Business Centre
Budbrooke Road
Warwick
CV34 5WE
England
Tel. 01926 499 619
Email: info@helion.co.uk
Website: www.helion.co.uk
Twitter: @helionbooks
Visit our blog http://blog.helion.co.uk/

Text © Adrien Fontanellaz 2022
Photographs © as individually credited
Colour artwork © Anderson Subtil, David
    Bocquelet and Luca Canossa 2022
Maps © Tom Cooper 2022

Designed and typeset by Farr out
    Publications, Wokingham, Berkshire
Cover design by Paul Hewitt, Battlefield
    Design (www.battlefield-design.co.uk)

ISBN 978-1-911628-66-8

British Library Cataloguing-in-Publication
    Data
A catalogue record for this book is available
    from the British Library

We always welcome receiving book
proposals from prospective authors.

CONTENTS

Note: To simplify the use of this book, all names, locations, and geographic designations are as provided in *The Times World Atlas*, or other traditional accepted major sources of reference, as of the time of described events. Mentions of Japanese individuals in this volume follow the Japanese convention, with family name coming first and given name second.

ABBREVIATIONS/GLOSSARY

AA	Anti-aircraft
AT	Anti-tank
AGS	(Imperial Japanese) Army General Staff
BAP	*Bombardirovochnyi Aviapolk* (Bomber regiment) (Soviet)
BGU	Border Garrison Unit
BT	*Bystrokhodny Tank* (Fast tank) (Soviet)
CAF	Chinese Air Force
CCP	Chinese Communist Party
CMC	Central Military Commission (parallel national defence organisation of the Communist Party of China)
CO	Commanding Officer
FAB	*Fugassnaya Aviobomba* (air-dropped bomb) (Soviet)
HQ	Headquarters
HMG	Heavy Machine Gun. In Japanese terminology, this included 7.7mm calibre machine guns which were classified as heavy
IAP	*Istrebitelnyi Aviapolk* (fighter regiment) (Soviet)
IGU	Independent Garrison Unit
IJA	Imperial Japanese Army
IJAAC	Imperial Japanese Army Air Corps
Kantogun	Kwantung Army
KIA	Killed in Action
KMT	Kuomintang of China (also 'Guomindang'; the Nationalist Party of China or the Chinese Nationalist Party)
Hiko Chutai	Flying or Air Company (6 to 12 aircraft)
Hiko Daitai	Flying or Air Battalion, usually composed of two companies
Hiko Dan	Flying or Air Brigade, composed of several Sentai and independent companies
Hiko Rentai	Flying or Air Regiment, usually composed of two battalions
Hiko Sentai	Flying Regiment, from mid-1938 on. Usually composed of three companies. Known colloquially as "Sentai"
Hiko Shidan	Flying or Air Division, composed of several brigades
LMG	Light Machine Gun
MIA	Missing in action
MPRA	Mongolian People's Republic Army
OKDVA	*Otdelynaya Krasnoznamennaya Dalyanevosto Chnaya Armiya* (Separate Far Eastern Red Banner Army) (Soviet)
NKVD	*Narodnyy komissariat vnutrennikh del* (People's Commissariat for Internal Affairs, also in charge of guarding the borders) (Soviet)
NRA	National Revolutionary Army (the KMT's Army)
RKKA	*Raboche-Krest'yanski Krasnoi Armiyy* (Workers and Peasants Red Army, or more colloquially, the Red or Soviet Army)
SABR	*Smeshannaya Aviabrigada* (mixed air brigade)
SBAP	*Skorostnoy Bombardirovochnyi Aviapolk* (fast bomber regiment)
TBAP	*Tyazholy Bombardirovochnyi Aviapolk* (Heavy bomber air unit) (Soviet)
USA	United States of America
USSR	Union of Soviet Socialist Republics
VVS RKKA	*Voenno-Vozdushnye Sily Raboche Krestiyanskoy Krasnoy Armii* (Military Air Forces of the Workers and Peasants Red Army) (Soviet). Known more colloquially as VVS

ADDENDUM/ERRATA FOR VOLUME 1

A recently published biography of the Soviet marshals serving under Stalin mentions that the trespassing and the setting of outposts in contested territory in the Lake Khasan area by NKVD border troops in July 1938 incensed Marshall Blyukher. Having given such orders, the same marshal was instrumental in attempting to keep the incident localised while concurrently attempting to re-seize the hills captured by the IJA 19th Division on 31 July. This was despite the unreadiness of the 39th Rifle Corps and all the while operating under tremendous pressure from Stalin. This transcript of a phone conversation taking place on 1 August 1938 between Blyukher and Stalin demonstrates the intents of the Soviet leader in relation to the incident:

> Comrade Blyukher, tell me honestly, as it befits a Communist, do you really have the desire to fight against the Japanese? If so, you will go there immediately. I don't understand your fear of the risks of your bombing operation, hitting the Korean population, nor the excuse that the weather is unfavourable to air missions.

> [...] Our main objective is to not allow the Japanese to remain on our territory. Nobody is forcing you to cross the border. We recommend only that you use our air force to bomb the Japanese to prevent them from gaining even a brief foothold on our territory.[1]

Blyukher was already a marked man, and on 31 August during a meeting of the Red Army Military Council he was accused of having failed dismally during the battle at Lake Khasan. Indeed, it was noted that "The combat direction by Blyukher during the Lake Khasan conflict was extremely unsatisfactory and bordered on conscious defeatism. All his behaviour at the onset or during the hostilities can only be described as duplicity, lack of discipline and sabotage of the actions undertaken to repulse the enemy."[2] The Marshall was expelled from the Army the same day and arrested on 22 October. He died under torture on 9 November 1938.[3]

According to Bulgarian historian Dimitiar Nedialkov, the VVS order of battle during the Lake Khasan battle included the

48th Shturmovaya Aviabrigada (R-10, SSS and R-5 aircraft), the *69th Iztrebitelnaya Aviabrigada* (I-15bis and I-16) and the *25th Skorostnaya Bombardirovachnaya Aviabrigada* as well as several independent reconnaissance squadrons. The TB-3 bombers engaged in the battle were from the 3rd AON. The VVS flew a total of 1,209 combat sorties during the incident, dropping 1,592 bombs and firing 37,985 MG rounds in the process. One SB-2 and one I-15bis were shot down by the Japanese and another two I-15bis crash-landed after having been damaged by the same. Of note was a massive raid on 6 August 1938 involving a wave of 41 TB-3, followed by 89 SB-2 and 30 I-15bis, the latter being tasked to strafe Japanese anti-aircraft batteries. Another 25 I-16 were escorting these formations although the carefully orchestrated air strike fell into confusion because of the bad weather.[4]

Preface

Those interested in the Second World War will know that during the spring and summer of 1939 – the very eve of the war erupting in Europe – Soviet and Japanese forces battled with each other within the confines of Manchuria and Mongolia, and that the Japanese were heavily defeated at the hands of the Soviet Army. The 129-day-long campaign had wide-ranging consequences even though it has remained unstudied until recently. Firstly, the Nomonhan Incident itself was of tremendous importance for Moscow as it could not afford to show any sign of weakness while conducting the complex and crucial set of negotiations which led to the signature of the Treaty of Non-Aggression between Germany and the Union of Soviet Socialist Republics, known more colloquially as the Molotov–Ribbentrop Pact signed on 19 August 1939. The heavy defeat suffered at the hands of the Soviets dampened the Imperial Japanese Army's appetite for a war with the Soviet Union and contributed heavily into Tokyo switching more and more toward the so-called "Southern Road" doctrine, i.e., an expansion in Southeast Asia, instead of the "Northern" option, targeting foremost the Soviet Union, and traditionally advocated by the Army. This in turn led to the signature on 13 April 1941 of the Soviet-Japanese Neutrality Pact which, crucially, eliminated the prospect of Japan invading the Russian Far East in the wake of Operation Barbarossa. Moscow thus avoided a potentially fatal war fought on two fronts.

Another crucial facet of this conflict is that it allowed an until-then unknown commander – Gueorgui Konstantinovitch Zhukov – to gain crucial experience of war and Stalin's trust. This was to be of paramount importance a few years later once the Soviet Union fought for its very survival in the face of a German onslaught. In a sense, the Khalkin Gol Battle provided almost a preview of what would follow during the Great Patriotic War. Unprepared Soviet forces followed a swift learning curve before defeating their enemy thanks to a markedly superior conduct of operations against an opponent perceiving itself as intrinsically superior. This lesson was however largely ignored, if only because it was overshadowed by the dismal performance of the Soviet Army during the war against Finland which began only three months later. The Nomonhan Incident also demonstrated the ineptness of the Japanese Army doctrine despite it being tailor-made for such a conflict. Indeed, it was so embodied in, and so related to, the core beliefs of the institution that this was largely ignored. The Japanese Army did, however, learn several lessons from the incident and they prompted the adoption of a new, more powerful, anti-tank gun, and encouraged the Imperial Japanese Air Corps into acquiring new fighter designs. These designs emphasised speed and firepower over sheer manoeuvrability thus paving the way for the induction of aircraft such as the Ki-44 or the Ki-61.

As is the case with the first volume in this mini-series, the reader should be forewarned that the battle that will be described is mainly viewed from a Japanese perspective; foremost because English-language documentation relevant to the battle is much more readily available, and secondly thanks to the existence of the US Army commissioned monographs recording Japanese operations plus a series of instrumental works such as those of Alvin D. Coox. He dedicated a lifetime of study to the Changkufeng and Nomonhan incidents detailing them minutely while interviewing hundreds of Japanese veterans in the process. As always, such an endeavour would not have been possible without the support and contributions of several individuals. The author would therefore like to thank Albert Grandolini for granting the use of pictures from his extensive collection, Tom Cooper, as always, for his invaluable advice and the Helion team for its support and hard work which made the coming into being of this book possible. In particular, the author would like to thank Stephen Rookes for his critical review and editing of the manuscript.

INTRODUCTION

The end of the nineteenth century saw the rise of two powers in the Far East; these being the Empires of Russia and Japan that soon began a competition to expand their sphere of influence (mostly to the detriment of China and Korea) until they found themselves engulfed in a bloody war in 1904. The conflict ended in a Japanese victory, even though this was largely the result of the civil unrest which erupted in Russia rather than the, all too real, series of successes on the battlefield gained at a high cost by the Japanese. This resulted in both empires sharing their influence on Manchuria, an integral part of the decaying Chinese Empire, and ruled by the Qin Dynasty. Indeed, the latter fell in 1911 and the country became a Republic. However, this only accelerated the centrifugal forces that had been active for decades. Before long, and while remaining nominally united, the new Republic soon became divided into semi-independent dominions ruled by local warlords of various strength and independence and allied into several cliques struggling for dominance. This division paved the way for several episodes of civil war during the 1920s. In Russia in 1917, the Tsarist regime was brought down resulting in this immense country entering a vicious civil war opposing the "Whites" – a disparate array of conservative and liberal forces – and the "Reds" or Communist forces. The latter, emerging victorious, inherited an utterly devastated but united land. In the meantime, the Japanese made the most of the First Word War. The economy was booming, and this facilitated Japan's seizure of former German possessions in Asia. On the other hand, Tokyo went too far by attempting, in 1915, to bully China into submitting to unacceptable concessions, these being the so-called "21 Demands". An expeditionary force was sent to Siberia in 1919 with the nominal objective of supporting the Whites. Nonetheless, a primary objective consisted of establishing a foothold in the Russian Far East. Both ventures ended in failure: the 21 Demands had to be withdrawn in the face of fierce Chinese and also Western opposition, while the Siberian endeavour ended with the withdrawal of the last Japanese troops in 1922.

The 1920s proved to be far more peaceful than the preceding decade. Japan was ruled by liberal politicians

A Russian artillery battery on the move during the Russo-Japanese War. (Albert Grandolini Collection)

pursuing international economic cooperation policies rather than old-fashioned imperialist ones, and this was to ensure the prosperity of the empire while the Bolsheviks were focusing on the construction of the Soviet Union and avoiding military engagement against other powers. China was also largely inactive on the international scene because it was engulfed in a series of civil wars waged by several coalitions of warlords. During these, the Kuomintang (KMT) gradually consolidated its hold over the country. This was achieved either by defeating its enemies outright or by rallying an increasing number of warlords to fight by its side. Nevertheless, the seeds of another civil war were soon to be sown when the KMT turned against its Communists allies in 1927. Despite being decimated, the Chinese Communist Party (CCP) not only managed to survive but also expanded by establishing control over several sanctuary areas. By the early 1930s, the KMT was engaged into waging a series of – unsuccessful – "encirclement" campaigns against the CCP, assessing it to be its most dangerous foe in the long run.

The Conquest of Manchuria

Indeed, the early 1930s were to mark a return toward belligerence, especially in Japan. Repeated economic downturns – foremost the Great Depression – and the existence of several competing cores of ultra-nationalist hard-liners were to put traditional political elites under increasing pressure to the point where it eventually folded after a series of assassinations and attempted coups carried out by the radical factions. This pressure was exerted especially by the Imperial Japanese Navy and the Imperial Japanese Army (IJA) To add salt to the wound the IJA itself was plagued with a distinctly Japanese, and endemic, form of insubordination known as *Gekokujo*. This allowed relatively junior officers to act by their own volition, even to the point of starting a war provided they were convinced it was for the greater good of the Japanese empire. The IJA's dysfunctional command structure failed over and over to assert its authority over these mavericks, and they were to find themselves in a position whereby they could repeatedly dictate national policy. This was

Tanks of the IJA's 2nd Independent Tank Company in Shanghai in 1932. In the foreground we see a Type 89 Medium Tank and, in the background, a French Renault NC-29. (Albert Grandolini Collection)

apanese soldiers pose on a camel during the invasion of Manchuria in
931. (Albert Grandolini Collection)

especially because the Imperial government – and even the emperor
himself – failed to assert their authority over the armed forces.

In 1919, the IJA activated the Kantogun, or Kwantung Army,
nitially a divisional-sized command, to protect both the Liaodong
Peninsula that Japan had inherited from the Russo-Japanese War, as
well as the infrastructures of the Japanese-owned *Minami Manshu
Tetsudo Kabushiki Kaisha* (South Manchurian Railway). Of crucial
mportance was that the Kwantung Army embodied *Gekokujo*,
and several of its officers began to meddle in Chinese politics,
noticeably by supporting Marshall Chang Tso-Lin, an astute and
powerful warlord who had managed to carve his own dominion
by establishing control over Manchuria. In 1928, however, several
Kwantung Army officers had become disillusioned with Chang
Tso-Lin and assassinated him, thus committing a blunder of major
proportions, Chang Tso-Lin was succeeded by his son, Marshall
Chang Hsueh-liang. Proving to be even less malleable than his
father, he entered an allegiance with the KMT then attempted to
re-establish control over the Soviet-owned Chinese Eastern Railway
in July 1929. This in turn triggered a three-month-long war with the
Soviet Union between October and December 1929 that resulted in
defeat to the Soviet Special Far Eastern Army.

In turn this worried to no end a coterie of Kwantung Army officers
who, for separate reasons, were determined to place Manchuria
under Japanese domination. They plotted an outright invasion of
the region, and it took place between September 1931 and February
1932 with both the IJA and then the Japanese government being
forced to endorse it and dispatch reinforcements to support the
Kwantung Army operations. On their own initiative Japanese
officers furthermore triggered the so-called First Shanghai Incident
by way of creating a diversion. This led to two months of vicious
urban fighting between Japanese and Chinese forces. Between 1932
and 1934 Manchuria was transformed into a nominally independent
state (the Empire of Manchukuo) ruled by Henry Pu Yi, the last
Qing Emperor. Controlled in essence by the Kwantung Army, the
new state became more and more a Japanese economic colony and
proved to be essential to the supply of an ever-increasing influx of
raw materials to the metropolis. However, this exercise in state-
building was not popular with the local Chinese populations and
before long numerous Kwantung Army forces had become engaged
in an almost never-ending and vicious "anti-bandit" struggle and
were increasingly reliant on the local Manchukuoan army raised
mostly for this purpose.

The China Incident

Almost as soon as Manchuria was secured, a series of *Gekokujo*
occurred with either Japanese troops or proxy forces attempting
to expand Japanese influence toward Northern China or Inner
Mongolia. At first, Chiang Kai-shek, the KMT supremo, refrained
from escalating the would-be conflicts and compromised with the
Japanese. This was due to the struggle against the CCP still being
a priority. At the same time, the building-up of a Nationalist army
strong enough to fight the Japanese was far from being achieved
despite the support of a small German advisory mission. However,
Chiang Kai-shek was also under increasing pressure from an incensed
Chinese public and from several powerful KMT figures to conclude
a truce with the Communists and form a united front against the
Japanese. By early 1937 continuing to appease the Japanese was not
politically feasible anymore. This said, hot-headed Japanese officers
and officials failed to notice this crucial development. Thus, things
quickly went out of control when, on 7 July 1937, an incident opposed
local Chinese and Japanese forces on the Marco Polo Bridge on the
outskirts of Peking. Within weeks, several IJA divisions launched a
general advance into Northern China while, in August, the KMT
escalated the conflict by opening a second front in Shanghai. Here,
its forces attempted to liquidate the Japanese concession. In turn,
this led to the dispatch of IJA reinforcements, and a three-month-
long battle of attrition that certainly ended with the decimation of
the best Nationalist troops, but also at unexpectedly high price for
the Japanese. The Shanghai battle won, the Japanese rushed toward
Nanking, the Nationalist capital. Here, on 13 December, their troops
captured the city opening the stage for a three-week-long orgy of
murder, rape and other exactions that claimed the lives of at least
200,000 Chinese civilians and prisoners of war.

Next followed a series of large-scale operations during 1938,
foremost the Wuhan Operations, the IJA attempted to break the
KMT's will to resist, but to no avail. Despite staggering advances
over huge distances, a succession of tactical victories and extremely
heavy losses inflicted on the enemy, the Japanese campaigns failed to
force the KMT into surrendering. On the contrary, the Nationalists'
morale fuelled from time-to-time by local victories against the
invaders, simply withdrew further and further into continental
China. Even Japanese attempts to cut their supply lines with the
outside world failed to convince them that they would not win by
remaining in the game in the long run. By early 1939, it had become
obvious that Japan had placed itself in an inextricable quagmire of
its own making: 25 of its divisions were fighting in China leaving
92,000 soldiers dead and another 216,000 wounded since the
beginning of the war. To make the situation worse, there was no
prospect of ending the so-called "Chinese Incident".

As this photo shows, the Japanese were enthusiastic users of armoured trains, and used them extensively during the invasion of Manchuria and the Chinese Incident. (Albert Grandolini Collection)

A Chinese 75mm Bofors AA gun in the vicinity of Chongqing. In a sense, this is a deceptive image as the Nationalists were hopelessly short on heavy weaponry of all kinds. The Japanese benefitted from a major advantage in firepower throughout the war. (Albert Grandolini Collection)

Increasing Tensions

The presence of Japanese forces in Manchuria had, in the meantime, compelled the Kremlin to reinforce the *Otdelynaya Krasnoznamennaya Dalyanevosto Chnaya Armiya* (OKVDA), or Separate Far Eastern Red Banner Army, a force tasked to defend the Far Eastern regions of Russia. Japanese intelligence assessed that these forces grew from six rifle divisions and two cavalry brigades in 1931, to 24 rifle divisions in 1938, supported by 1,500 aircraft and 1,500 tanks.[1] This build-up of the OKVDA proved possible only because the Soviet Union had made enormous efforts to expand its armed forces, foremostly the *Raboche-Krest'yanski Krasnoi Armiyy* (RKKA), or Workers and Peasants Red Army. Moscow, therefore, not only expanded its heavy industries at a frenetic pace but used these capabilities to produce unheard off quantities of weaponry, some of which, particularly tanks, were designed using help from the West.

Crucially, the Soviets intended to build-up massive quantities of mechanised forces able to operate according to their "Deep Battle" and "Deep Operation" doctrines. This is where mobile and armoured units would operate in a series of sequenced operations in enemy territory, eventually dismantling the opponent's ability to wage war. For the same reason, the Soviets proved to be forerunners as regards of the creation of airborne forces while building a powerful air force. In a nutshell, Moscow was mobilising the entire nation into building a gigantic and well-equipped army able to operate according to what was arguably the most advanced doctrine of the time. This, however, did not worry the Japanese officer corps. On the contrary, over the previous two decades the IJA had developed a doctrine whereby a well-trained and aggressive infantry was to compensate for the numerical and material superiority of the enemy, intended to defeat the RKKA through a series of decisive victories gained through fast-paced mobile operations that relied mostly on intangible factors such as a supposed uniquely Japanese fighting spirit.

Unsurprisingly, incidents became common along the 4,700-kilometre-long border shared by the two powers. This included that between Manchukuo and the Mongolian People's Republic as the latter was a Soviet satellite defended by Soviet troops from at least 1936. Until 1937, the Soviets showed restraint as Moscow was wary of an all-out war against Japan while tensions in Europe were on the rise. Reaching the point whereby the Japanese got away with sinking a Soviet gunboat on the Amur River in early July 1937, the tables were finally turned a few weeks later once the Japanese engaged themselves in all-out war in China, and therefore lost the ability to attack the Soviet Union provided the conflict continued. Of course, Moscow made the most of this opportunity by supporting the KMT with massive deliveries of weapons and ammunition of all sorts; and even by dispatching combat pilots and advisers to China to help the beleaguered Chinese to sustain their war effort.

Rather unsurprisingly, the next major border incident turned into something entirely different. This took place at the end of July 1938 on Manchukuoan soil, albeit in an area under the auspices of the Japanese *Chosengun* (Korea Army). Following a series of skirmishes, in a battle lasting 10 days the IJA's 19th Division fought the entire RKKA 39th Rifle Corps to gain control over a series of commanding heights located in a loop between the Tumen River and Lake Khasan. Benefiting from its control over the heights (the Changkufeng and Shachaofeng Hills), the 19th Division managed to inflict a total of 3,544 casualties, losing 1,439 casualties out of the 6,814 men directly engaged in the battle in the process. This meant that it was barely able to keep its positions in the face of repeated and determined Soviet attacks.

Both sides proving unwilling to escalate the situation, the "Battle of Lake Khasan", (the Changkufeng Incident to the Japanese), ended with a ceasefire on 11 August. Indeed, the Japanese eventually withdrew from the area leaving the Soviets to take control of the contested hills a few days later and leaving them victorious in anything but name. As for the Japanese, they were content to have tested the waters and to have ascertained that Moscow was not interested in intervening directly to support the Chinese. This left them with a free hand to initiate the Wuhan Operation that was expected to end the war in China. Importantly, the IJA, and the Kwantung Army in particular, failed to draw any significant lessons from the Changkufeng incident. This was the case with their massive inferiority regarding artillery as this paved the way for a much more dramatic confrontation which was to take place one year later on almost the opposite side of Manchuria.

1

A GREEN DIVISION

Whereas the Kwantung Army perceived itself largely as the very best force in the Imperial Japanese Army, its officer corps was renowned for its propensity for unruly behaviour towards the Army General Staff (AGS) in Tokyo. Apart from its position as a military command, the Kwantung Army played a key role in Manchukuoan politics – the Army had a reputation for being a hotbed of *Gekokujo*. Since 1936, it had been commanded by General Ueda Kenkichi, a veteran of both the Siberia Expedition and the First Shanghai Incident during which he commanded the 9th Division. His Chief of Staff was Lieutenant General Ieogai Reneuke, a well experienced combat leader who previously served as commander of the 10th Division in China. Particularly decisive in the Kwantung Army decision-making process was the Staff 1st Section,[1] in charge of operations, led by Colonel Terada Masao. This unit included three other key figures; Lieutenant Colonel Murasawa Kasuo, Major Tsuji Masanobu and Major Shimanuki Takeji. Of these four officers, Major Tsuji Masanobu, reputedly a hyperactive maverick, was the best acquainted with local conditions, therefore holding a significant influence over the others. Overall, the Kwantung Army Staff at the time was largely perceived as a cohesive and tightly knit group.

The Kwantung Army's main mission was to defend Manchuria against the Soviets while preparing for an all-out war when, in this case, it would be reinforced by the bulk of the IJA. Though it had already begun to prepare for the ambitious Otsu plan,

its implementation was unsuitable before the end of the Chinese Incident or, in any case, not before 1943. In the meantime, the Kwantung Army made plans to face up to the possibility of a Soviet offensive by counterattacking on the eastern (Ussuri) front once reinforcements became available. Meanwhile, defensive positions were to be kept in place on the northern (Amur) front and in Western Manchuria.

Accordingly, the 3rd Army, in charge of the Ussuri Front, was the strongest with three divisions and three Border Garrison Units (BGU), while the weaker 4th and 5th Armies oversaw holding the line or making a fighting withdrawal. Consequently, the 4th Army comprised one division and three BGU, while the 5th Army was made up of one division, one cavalry brigade and one BGU.

Soldiers of the 23rd Division disembarking from their trucks. As with all other Japanese divisions, the infantry moved on foot. (Albert Grandolini Collection)

Soldiers set up field communication lines. Japanese field units suffered from an endemic lack of reliable radios. Correspondingly, field phones and messengers played a crucial role. (Albert Grandolini Collection)

siege of Port Arthur in the Russo-Japanese War. It was a classically structured IJA division comprising two brigades made up of two infantry regiments. The Division was at peace time strength with each of its 12 infantry battalions including three infantry companies instead of four.[2]

Operational Order No. 1488

By early 1939, the Kwantung Army Staff had grown dissatisfied with their perceived soft-handed handling of both the 1937 Amur Incident – the 1st Division being refrained from escalating the conflict – and the Changkufeng incident during which the contested area was abandoned to the Soviets. In particular, the AGS had refused a proposal whereby the Kwantung Army was to launch an offensive to regain the lost ground. In the eyes of the Staff 1st Bureau, this demonstrated a lack of aggressiveness in the face of provocations on the Soviet border, and it was bound to encourage them to be even more brazen in the future.

Accordingly, to make sure that local IJA commanders would react with the desired determination and not let the higher strata of the IJA hierarchy meddle in its affairs, a new Kwantung Army operation order, the "Principles for the Settlement of Soviet-Manchukuoan Border Disputes" was issued on 25 April 1939 to serve as a guideline when such occasions arose. In short, local commanders were to be free to determine the threat and, more importantly, to repulse trespassers with armed force without worrying about the consequences. As the Principles made crystal clear: "If the enemy crosses the border [he should be] annihilated without delay using forces carefully built up beforehand. If the enemy violates the borders, friendly units must challenge him courageously and endeavour to triumph in their zone of action without concerning themselves with the consequences that are the responsibility of the higher command."[3]

A Unique Division

One of the most recent additions to the Kwantung Army was the 23rd Division, a relatively new force raised in April 1938 in Kyushu Island. Both Lieutenant General Komatsubura Michitaro, its CO and Colonel Ouchi Tsutomu, its Chief of Staff, were considered as Soviet experts with the former speaking Russian and having served as a military attaché in Moscow. However, neither of them was considered as "combat leaders". In July of the same year, the new regular division was assigned to the Kwantung Army and dispatched to Hailar where it replaced a divisional-sized Cavalry Group that had been sent to China. The 23rd Division HQ also took over control of the local 8th BGU, a fortress unit composed of four infantry battalions, one artillery regiment and one engineer battalion (7,000 men in total) tasked with defending the town and its surrounding areas.

The Manchukuoan army was also present in Hailar. This town harboured the HQ of the Hsingan Cavalry Division made up of four cavalry regiments, two artillery batteries (a total of 1,851 men), while another three cavalry

As for command over operations, the Kwantung Army HQ had direct control over the 4th Division which was given the mission of defending the Chiamussu area, the 23rd Division, tasked with defending the Hailar area, five Independent Guard Units, as well as a strategic reserve including the 1st Tank Group, with two tank regiments, and the 7th Division. Nicknamed the "Bear Division", this unit founded on 19 July 1896 in Hokkaido was widely assessed as one of the best in the IJA due to its distinguishing itself at the

A battery of Type 38 Howitzers of the 13th Field Artillery Regiment. By 1939, these were utterly obsolete weapons. (Albert Grandolini Collection)

Table 1: Kwantung Army order of battle as of May 1939	
4th Division	HQ Chiamussu
7th Division	HQ Tsitsihar, act as Kwantung Army strategic reserve
23rd Division	HQ Hailar, controls the 8th BGU
1st Independent Garrison Unit	HQ Mukden, 1st to 6th Independent Garrison Infantry Battalions
2nd Independent Garrison Unit	HQ Hsinking, 7th to 12th Independent Garrison Infantry Battalions
3rd Independent Garrison Unit	HQ Angangchi, 13th to 18th Independent Garrison Infantry Battalions
4th Independent Garrison Unit	HQ Mutanchiang, 19th to 24th Independent Garrison Infantry Battalions
5th Independent Garrison Unit	HQ Harbin, 25th to 30th Independent Garrison Infantry Battalions
3rd Field Heavy Artillery Brigade	Two artillery regiments
1st Tank Group	HQ Kungchuling, 3rd and 4th Tank Regiments
3rd Army	HQ Mutanchiang, 2nd 8th and 12th divisions, 1st, 2nd, and 3rd Border Garrisons Units
4th Army	HQ Peian, 1st Division, 5th, 6th and 7th Border Garrisons Units
5th Army	HQ Tungan, 11th Division, 3rd Cavalry Brigade, 4th Border Garrison Unit

Table 2: IJA's 7th "Bear" Division as of May 1939	
Unit	CO
Division HQ	Lieutenant General Kunisaki Noburu
13th Brigade HQ	Major General Yoshizawa Tadao
25th Infantry Regiment	Colonel Sekine Kyutaro
26th Infantry Regiment	N/A
14th Brigade HQ	Major General Morita Norimasa
27th Infantry Regiment	Colonel Sannomiya Mitsuji
28th Infantry Regiment	Colonel Ashizuka Chozo
7th Field Artillery Regiment	Colonel Hirayama Yoshiro
7th Cavalry Regiment	Lieutenant Colonel Akiyama Kyuzo
7th Engineer Regiment	Lieutenant Colonel Yokoyama Yoshitomo
7th Transport Regiment	Lieutenant Colonel Honma Kotaro

Trucks of the 23rd Transport Regiment. The few dozen available vehicles of this type proved wholly insufficient to transform the 23rd Division into even a marginally motorised force. (Albert Grandolini Collection)

regiments, two artillery batteries and one armoured car unit (2,936 men in total) were garrisoned in Chen-chiatien. Some distance away was the Chingan Infantry Division. This comprised three infantry regiments, two cavalry regiments, two artillery regiments, (2,552 men in total) garrisoned in Mukden and Tsitsihar.

These forces – the 23rd Division in particular – were tasked with defending the western confines of Manchuria, but they were to be found low on the list of priorities for the Kwantung Army. The reason for this was explained by Lieutenant Colonel Hattori Takuahiro, a former head of its staff operations section:

In its plan of operations against the USSR in 1939, the Kwantung Army had no offensive plans toward the western border, i.e., towards Hailar, Arshaan, or the western Outer Mongolia area. At that time, in the event of a war breaking out between Japan and the USSR, we estimated that the main area of conflict in Manchuria would be around the eastern border, so the Kwantung Army was to prepare to hold out in the west with minimum strength. Directly after the commencement of a war, it could naturally be expected that a powerful Soviet force would thrust against the Hailar area. Against this, our only forces were the 23rd Division and the Hailar border defence garrison. It was to be expected, then, that warfare in this area would, within a short

period, develop into our being surrounded by the powerful Soviet Army. As for us, we therefore had to erect circular fortifications on the heights around Hailar and prepare to fight to the last. Completely on the defensive, thus absorbing the enemy thrust and accomplishing our objective of holding out, overall, we limited our commitment to the smallest possible factor. Perhaps, we were risking even less than the minimum hence the operational orders being entirely defensive.[4]

The assignment of the 23rd Division to Hailar was motivated by its lack of combat readiness and its limited ability to conduct offensive operations. Indeed, the IJA considered that such a newly raised unit needed at least a year and a half of training to be assessed as fully combat-ready, and even by May 1939, the division was almost one year short of this. Worse, the division's cohesiveness had been affected by the garrisoning of several sub-units away from Hailar because the latter did not have the necessary accommodation for the entire unit, and the winter of 1938-1939 limited field manoeuvres. The division was commanded by experienced men, but a number of junior officers had only just been commissioned or they had come from the reserves and lacked experience of combat.

Lieutenant General Komatsubura Michitaro (left). (Albert Grandolini Collection)

An armoured car crew of 57th KON proudly pose in front of their vehicle. (Albert Grandolini Collection)

A squad of MPRA troopers listening to the orders of their commanding officer. They are armed with Mosin Nagant rifles and a single DP-28 LMG. (Albert Grandolini Collection)

The 23rd Division being among the first triangular divisions raised by the IJA, it was therefore made up of a single brigade HQ,[5] three infantry regiments, as well as the other usual supporting units (a total of 14,072 men and 2,358 horses). To increase its mobility, and its ability to operate in the plains of Western Manchuria, the transport regiment was assigned a motorised transport company with 32 trucks. This was soon followed by a second transport unit while the reconnaissance regiment had one cavalry company and one armoured company with a dozen Type 94 tankettes instead of the usual two cavalry companies.

By that time, the IJA was, however, chronically short of heavy weapons: industry could barely keep up with the demands of the war in China that coincided with the raising of new units. As a result, the three battalions of the 13th Field Artillery Regiment were equipped with 24 unmodernised Type 38 75mm field guns plus 12 Type 38 120mm Field Howitzers – the Japanese versions of the 1903 Krupp L/30 field gun and 1905 Krupp L/12 field howitzer respectively. These obsolete weapons were particularly ill-suited to the theatre as range of the Type 38 120mm field howitzer was limited to roughly five kilometres. Faced with these limitations, once the 23rd Division was ordered to move to the battle zone at the end of June 1939 the unit's chief of ordnance, Colonel Chikazawa, shot himself out of shame.

Despite the plains being obviously ideal "tank country", the 23rd Division was only able to muster 12 Type 94 37mm AT guns and the 12 Type 41 75mm infantry guns divided equally between the three infantry regiments. Unsurprisingly, the divisional manoeuvres held during the winter of 1938-1939

BT-7 fast tanks, and one of the very few SU-1 self-propelled guns ever produced, of the 57th KON during manoeuvres. The SU-1 consisted of a 76mm M1927 regimental gun mounted on a GAZ-AAA truck. (Albert Grandolini Collection)

Table 3: The 23rd Division of the IJA, May 1939

Unit	CO	Notes
Division HQ	Lieutenant General Komatsubara Michitaro, Chief of Staff; Colonel Ouchi Tsutomu	
23rd Brigade HQ	Major General Kobayashi Koichu	
64th Infantry Regiment	Colonel Yamagata Takemitsu	Three battalions with four infantry companies, one MG company and a battalion gun platoon each
71st Infantry Regiment	Colonel Okamoto Tokuzo	Three battalions with four infantry companies, one MG company and a battalion gun platoon each
72nd Infantry Regiment	Colonel Sakai Mikio	Two battalions with four infantry companies, one MG company and a battalion gun platoon each
13th Field Artillery Regiment	Colonel Ise Takahide	Three battalions with nine batteries of four guns between them, equipped with 24 Type 38 75mm field guns and 12 Type 38 120mm Howitzers
23rd Reconnaissance Regiment	Lieutenant Colonel Azuma Yaozo	One cavalry company, one tankette company with 12 Type 94s, two motorised infantry companies, one motorised transport company
23rd Engineer Regiment	Lieutenant Colonel Saito Isamu	
23rd Transport Regiment	Lieutenant Colonel Midorikawa Chuji	1st Transport company (Horse) and 2nd Transport company (Trucks)

Table 4: 57th KON, Spring 1939

Units	Locality	Notes
HQ	Ulan Bator	CO Komdiv N.V. Feklenko
36th Motorised Rifle Division	Soin Shanda	CO Major I.P. Dorofeev. 24th, 76th and 149th Motorised Rifle Regiments, 175th Artillery Regiment, one Tank Battalion
6th Cavalry Brigade	Yugodzyr	143rd and 155th Cavalry Regiments, 39th Horse Artillery Regiment
11th Tank Brigade	Undur Khan	CO Kombrig M.P. Yakovlev. 16th, 24th, 45th Tank Battalions, 175th Rifle Machine-Gun Battalion, 354th Artillery Battalion, 335th Auto-mobile Battalion
7th Motor-Mechanised Brigade	Dzamin-Ude	CO Major A.A. Lesovoy. 247th Armoured Battalion, 161st Rifle Machine-Gun Battalion, 204th Reconnaissance Battalion
8th Motor-Mechanised Brigade	Bain Tumen	CO Colonel V.A. Mishulin. 234th Armoured Battalion, 164th Tank Battalion, 171st Rifle Machine-Gun Battalion, 223rd Reconnaissance Battalion
9th Motor-Mechanised Brigade	Ulan Bator	CO Colonel S.I. Oleynikov. 241st Armoured Battalion, 196th Rifle Machine-Gun Battalion, 240th Reconnaissance Battalion

Special Assignment Corps

In the aftermath of the Changkufeng Incident, Moscow dismantled the OKVDA and its CO, Marshall Blyukher, was executed on 9 November 1938. As a result, the 1st Red Banner Army took over the Ussuri Area, the 2nd Red Banner Army became responsible for the Amur Area, and further west, RKKA forces remained under the aegis of the Trans-Baikal Military District. All of these reported directly to the People's Defence National Commissariat in Moscow. Together, these three commands were estimated by the Japanese to contain a total of 24 rifle divisions, 2,000 aircraft and 1,900 tanks.[7]

On top of this, following the signing of the Soviet-Mongolian Mutual Assistance Pact in March 1936, the RKKA had activated the 57th KON (*Korpus Osobogo Naznacheniya*, or Special Assignment Corps) to control all Soviets units deployed in Mongolia. Its HQ was in Ulan Bator and was attached to the Trans-Baikal Military District. By spring 1939, the Corps had grown into a rather powerful, but still compact, mobile force with one motorised rifle division, one tank brigade, one cavalry brigade and three motor-mechanised brigades. These consisted of one battalion each of armour, rifle machine-gun, and reconnaissance as well as smaller support units comprising a total of 1,888 men, 82 armoured cars, 10 guns and 320 other vehicles. By then, the 57th KON had 27,500 men, 284 tanks, 370 other armoured vehicles and 200 guns with a calibre superior to 45mm. In essence, it was immensely superior in terms of numbers and firepower to the 23rd Division and was also

revealed that the division lacked both mobility and firepower; its combat effectiveness being rated as "below average".[6]

much better adapted to local conditions. Furthermore, the Corps was lavishly equipped as far as transport was concerned. Indeed, in February 1939, it had a total of 5,208 trucks, 872 light and specialised vehicles, 631 tankers, 245 mobile repair shops, 91 tractors and 265 motorcycles.[8]

The Soviets garrisoned in Mongolia could rely on the small Mongolian People's Revolutionary Army (MPRA). Comprising 20,000 men in 1939, it was equipped with Soviet material and trained along RKKA standards. The MPRA was in essence a cavalry force and was structured into two corps controlling a total of eight cavalry divisions plus a single – and badly understrength – armoured brigade. These divisions, numbered from 1 to 8, had a nominal 1,591 men and were in turn divided up into two cavalry regiments each

with one mounted machine gun squadron, a battalion of armoured cars (two squadrons of nine armoured cars each), and an artillery battalion using four M1902 or M1927 76mm guns and six M1932 45mm AT guns. Several divisions, however, were missing a full complement of heavy weaponry. While the MPRA was corseted by Soviet advisers, animosities between Mongolian and Soviet officers ran high, foremost because the latter were perceived as patronising by the former.[9]

2
YELLOW STARS AGAINST RED STARS

As was the case with the Manchukuoan-Soviet border, numerous segments of the Mongolian-Manchukuoan border were ill-defined or contested. Noticeably, this was the case at the tip of the north-eastern salient whereby Mongolian territory extended into Manchuria. According to the Manchukuoans and Japanese, the border followed the course of the Halha River ("Khalkin Gol" for both Mongolian and Soviets) but for the Mongolians and Soviets it started roughly 20 kilometres from the eastern bank of the river. The contested area east of the Halha included the small settlement of Nomonhan located 12 kilometres from the river. This was fertile ground for border incidents as both sides respected their own interpretation of what constituted the border. For the Japanese, the Mongolian forces operating east of the river were trespassing on Manchukuoan territory while for Mongolian forces it was the other way around.

The whole area east of the Halha River consisted of uninhabited, undulating, and sandy plains, partly covered with shrubs less than a metre in height on average. There were also numerous sand dunes, and ravines and hollow valleys which could reach a depth of as much as 40 metres, as well as a few heights but whose elevation did not exceed 40 to 50 metres. The latter were called "barkhans" by the Mongolians.

The terrain did not provide sufficient cover to hide a large number of troops or artillery positions, and although the sandy soil made the digging of trenches easy their sides had to be stabilised using wooden planks or galvanised sheet iron. The whole area was cut in two by the Holsten River (Hailastyn Gol for the Mongolians and Soviets), a tributary of the Halha River which ran from north to south. The river itself was only four metres wide and two metres deep, but it dissected a valley some 1.5 kms wide. Of crucial importance was the Halha River itself. It was 120 to 130 metres wide, two metres deep and had very few fordable points. The valley surrounding the river was one to three kilometres wide and extremely muddy. Crucially, the western side of the valley was 50 metres higher than the eastern side. This was to be of tremendous importance because this was to give both Mongolian and Soviet artillerymen an open field of view on the plains on the eastern side of the Halha while their Japanese counterparts could not sight them from their own positions. The climate was hot during the day and very cold during the night from April onwards while, as winter arrived in October, temperatures fell as low as minus 30 degrees Fahrenheit.

Unsurprisingly, the whole area was not well-connected in terms of communications infrastructure, but the Japanese held a distinct advantage in this regard as they had a railhead at Handagai, 80 kilometres from Hailar, the two localities being connected by three

distinct unpaved roads. Only dirt roads ran along the 160 kilometres separating Hailar from Nomonhan. On the other hand, the nearest Soviet railhead was in Borzya, around 640 kilometres from the Halha River.[1] Whereas the border area of Mongolia and Manchukuo was apparently devoid of any value, by 1939 both sides had grown aware of its potential strategic importance. The Soviets knew that a Japanese advance through Mongolia could potentially cut their Far Eastern Forces from Western Russia, and, in turn, the Kwantung Army long-term planning envisioned a massive offensive from Hailar toward the Trans-Baikal district with the Mongolian border flanking their advance.

The Tauran Incident

By early 1939, this part of the common border between Mongolia and Manchukuo had already been the scene of several incidents. These frequently involved Japanese forces of the Cavalry Group garrisoned at Hailar before the 23rd Division took over. By 1936, the Cavalry Group was composed of the 1st and 4th Cavalry Brigades with each comprising two cavalry regiments (13th and 14th for the 1st Cavalry Brigade, 25th and 26th for the 4th Cavalry Brigade) one horse artillery battery, a machine gun squadron, one engineer platoon, one tankette or cavalry tank company and a transport battalion.

On 11 January 1935, an 11-strong cavalry patrol of the Hsingan Cavalry Division clashed with a MPRA detachment northeast of Lake Buir losing its CO and suffering six wounded. MPRA forces seized the nearby small settlement of Halhamiao a few days later, and this prompted the Cavalry Group to dispatch a mixed detachment composed of two motorised companies, one MG company and a tankette platoon under Colonel Wada Yoshio, the CO of the 13th Cavalry Regiment. The Wada Detachment left Hailar on 27 January and covered the 200 kilometres separating it from Halhamiao in a single day. The settlement was reoccupied without a fight as the Mongolians had already withdrawn. Then, on 23 June 1935, a MPRA patrol captured a five-strong Japanese survey team travelling south of the confluence between the Halha and Holsten rivers. Once informed, the 1st Cavalry Brigade sent a cavalry company paired with an MG company under Major Yamazaki Takeshi. It, too, found that the Mongolians had vacated the area.

A far more serious incident occurred the following winter, again in the vicinity of Lake Buir. It began on 19 December 1935 when a Manchukuoan patrol clashed with a MPRA detachment southwest of the lake and was followed by a series of small-scale engagements from 8–6 January 1936 in the vicinity of Manchukuoan outposts in the same area. Whilst the Manchukuoans reported attacks by

MPRA cavalry and motorised forces against their positions, the MPRA mentioned having repulsed Manchukuoan detachments which had crossed the border on 15 January and 3 February with support of several air strikes flown by their R-5 light bombers. The IJA reacted to the incident on 8 February by dispatching from Hailar a mixed detachment from the 14th Cavalry Regiment led by Lieutenant Colonel Sugimoto Yasuo. It combined motorised infantry, cavalry units, a machine gun company, a tankette company, as well as a Manchukuoan cavalry detachment. On 12 February the Sugimoto detachment encountered a company sized MPRA force, and destroyed one enemy armoured car before withdrawing when coming under fire from Mongolian armoured cars. In turn, in early March, this prompted the Japanese to dispatch another detachment drawn from the 1st Independent Mixed Brigade, by then the only fully motorised unit in the entire IJA. The column was led by Colonel Shibuya Yasuaki and consisted of an infantry battalion reinforced by a tankette company and a mountain gun platoon. By the end of March, the Shibuya Detachment had arrived in the Lake Buir area, and between 29 and 30 March it took part in a series of skirmishes with an MPRA force of similar size including a cavalry regiment (roughly 300 men), a motorised infantry company, an artillery battery and a squadron of 10 armoured cars.

The two detachments clashed on 31 March with the Japanese getting a bloody nose. This was due, mostly, to the presence of the vastly superior enemy armoured cars and because Soviet and Mongolian crewed R-5s based in Bain Tumen flew several dozen missions. The fighting ending that same day, at its end the MPRA claimed to have inflicted 400 casualties and to have destroyed 40 vehicles, two tankettes and eight aircraft. Forced to withdraw, the Japanese acknowledged the loss of 13 men and two tankettes. However, they claimed to have captured a Mongolian armoured vehicle in the encounter. From that point, the so-called Tauran Incident did not escalate any further as the MPRA forces withdrew from the area.[2] The series of incidents around Lake Buir in early 1936 engendered serious consequences as it prompted Moscow to increase its involvement thus paving the way for the signature on 12 March 1936 of a Treaty of Mutual Assistance with Ulan Bator. With this, it dispatched RKKA reinforcements to Mongolia thus leading to the creation of the 57th KON.

Escalation

Thereafter, the Mongolian-Manchukuoan border remained relatively quiet, especially as from July 1937 the Japanese – their hands full with war against China – attempted not to become embroiled in further border incidents if it could be avoided. Nevertheless, the situation got out of control in the Nomonhan area in the spring of 1939, and on 4 May, a firefight occurred between a Manchukuoan patrol and elements of the MPRA's 200-strong 7th Border Guard Post, a unit responsible for control of the area. One Japanese NCO acting as an adviser was killed in the ensuing skirmish.

Another clash took place on 11 May, and here a Manchukuoan cavalry platoon encountered a 20-man MPRA patrol north of the Holsten River. The Mongolian force withdrew after having lost two men with one wounded, and as a result the 7th Border Guard Post's commander, Major Chogdan, dispatched 60 troops to the same area. They encountered the Manchukuoan platoon on 12 May and forced it to retreat. Simultaneously, Manchukuoan troops sent from Hailar fought against 700 Mongolian horsemen who had crossed the border and who threatened to overwhelm the 300 Manchukuoans present in this sector.

The 23rd Division HQ was informed of these clashes on 13 May, ironically the information arrived as Lieutenant General Komatsubara Michitaro chaired a meeting to discuss the implications of Operation Order 1488. Almost immediately, it was decided to send a detachment of the 23rd Reconnaissance Regiment commanded by Lieutenant Colonel Azuma Yaozo to the border area to repulse the MPRA trespassers. Its request for air support from Kwantung Army HQ was approved by General Ueda Kenkichi the following day. The 2nd Hiko Shidan (Air Division) dispatched to Hailar a composite air unit made up of one light bomber squadron from the 10th Sentai and two squadrons from the 24th Sentai. Totalling a force of 24 Ki-27 fighters and nine Ki-32 light bombers, the unit joined up with the 48th and 51st Airfield battalions. Two motorised transport companies from the 1st Transport Regiment were also dispatched and, on 14 May, a reconnaissance aircraft carrying Major Tsuji Masanobu overflew the Nomonhan sector. It did not spot any concentration of enemy forces but, nonetheless, it became clear that the MPRA was operating in the area upon the discovery of a bullet hole when the aircraft returned to base. In the meantime, the AGS approved the initiatives followed by the 23rd Division and Kwantung Army but warned them against any escalation.

During the next phase, the Azuma Detachment arrived in the Nomonhan area in the morning of 15 May. Made up of two infantry companies hastily motorised by using all the trucks available to the division, plus one cavalry troop and a tankette company, it arrived only to be informed by Manchukuoan horsemen present at the scene that the Mongolians had withdrawn to the other side of the Halha River.

The detachment nonetheless made a sweep toward the river but did not encounter any MPRA. Around midday, on the other

A trio of Japanese soldiers hastily entrenched in foxholes dug in the sandy ground. Of note is the Mauser pistol carried by one of the soldiers, most probably captured in China. (Albert Grandolini Collection)

A crucial mistake made by the Japanese was its failure to allocate anti-tank weapons such as the Type 94 rapid-fire guns to the 23rd Reconnaissance Regiment. (Albert Grandolini Collection)

Elements of the Yamagata Detachment group together on the eve of a battle fought on 28-29 May. (Albert Grandolini Collection)

Cavalrymen of the ill-fated 23rd Reconnaissance Regiment parading in front of the photographer. (Albert Grandolini Collection)

hand, Ki-32s of the 10th Sentai attacked the MPRA 7th Border Guard Post located on the western side of the Halha in uncontested Mongolian territory, carrying out bombing and strafing runs.

Two MPRA soldiers were killed and another 15 were wounded. Though this greatly increased the seriousness of the incident, unbothered by the consequences of its actions the Azuma Detachment left the area the following day and reached Hailar on 17 May.[3]

The Bykov Detachment

The attacks carried out by the 10th Sentai on 15 May prodded the proverbial hornet's nest. Over the following days, the entire 6th Cavalry Division (CO Colonel Shoaaiibuu) of the MPRA was sent to reinforce the 7th Border Guard Post. Comprising two cavalry regiments, its weapons included a four-gun battery of 76mm cannons, an armoured car squadron and a training company. The Soviets did not remain idle either. They dispatched the 11th Tank Brigade's 175th Rifle Machine-Gun Battalion including three rifle companies and eight T-37 tankettes reinforced with an armoured car company equipped with 16 BA-6, a reconnaissance platoon with another five armoured cars, an engineer company, a battery of AT guns and a battery of four SU-1 self-propelled guns and another of towed artillery. This powerful and mobile force of around 1,200 men was led by Major A.E Bykov. By the end of May, Mongolian and Soviet forces amounted to around 2,500 men, supported by at least twelve 76mm artillery pieces and nearly 40 armoured vehicles. The next stage was for engineers to build a bridge across the Halha River at a point north of its confluence with the Holsten River, and two miles west of Nomonhan they were instructed to construct a 15-kilometre-long defensive line east of and parallel to the river. It consisted mainly of a series of outposts and strongpoints manned by the 6th Cavalry Division's 15th and 17th Cavalry regiments. Two Soviet machine gun companies were positioned on the flanks of this line. A reserve made up of one machine-gun company, an engineer company as well as the available artillery was kept near the western end of the bridge.[4] Major Bykov described the operations as such:

> Following orders received from HQ, on 18 May my reconnaissance platoon the 6th Mongolian Cavalry Division were sent to the Hamardaba mountain range on the western bank of the Halha River. The first minor clash involving Soviet troops took place on 22 or 23 May when, in accordance with instructions from the Corps headquarters, I ordered my platoon to cross the Halha River to its eastern bank to collect information [...] My detachment arriving at the river on 24 May 1939, in accordance with my orders, on 26 May I sent two motorised rifle companies, a battery of 45-mm guns, and a few armoured cars across the river. On 27 May, I transferred our command post to the eastern bank of the Halha River, about 9-10 kms. from the state border line.[5]

Bis Repetita

As a matter of course the increased MPRA activity on the eastern bank of the Halha River was sighted by the Manchukuoan patrols monitoring the area and it was duly reported back to Hailar. On 22 May, a Manchukuoan cavalry regiment which had crossed the Soviet-claimed border line east of the Halha River was engaged by the BA-6s and BA-10s of Bykov's reconnaissance platoon – reinforced with other armoured cars – and was forced to withdraw after suffering heavy losses. The Manchukuoans did manage, nevertheless, to destroy four BA-6s, and this came as a result of the crews failing to mount auxiliary tracks and finding themselves bogged down in the sandy soil.

In response, Lieutenant General Komatsubara Michitaro dispatched a much stronger force under Colonel Yamagata Takemitsu (CO of the 64th Infantry Regiment) with the order to destroy enemy forces east of the Halha River. The Yamagata Detachment included the 64th Infantry Regiment's gun company and the 3rd Infantry Battalion, as well as Lieutenant Colonel Azuma's 23rd Reconnaissance Regiment, and three motorised transport companie, around 1,500 men in total. Colonel Yamagata could, furthermore, rely on the 1,200 troops of the Manchukuoan 1st, 7th and 8th Cavalry Regiments already in the area. By 23 May,

This image shows Japanese soldiers advancing at the double toward the enemy positions on 28 May 1939. (Albert Grandolini Collection)

Elements from three different Manchukuoan cavalry regiments took part in the battles of May 1939. (Albert Grandolini Collection)

the Yamagata Detachment had regrouped in Kanchuerhmiao, a town roughly 60 kilometres north of Nomonhan.

To confront enemy forces, Yamagata drew up a textbook IJA-style plan of attack: aggressive, and complex to the point of being almost elegant. Still, while the Japanese knew that the enemy had built a bridge across the river, they had only a hazy picture of the number of enemy forces and their positions. Effectively, they had absolutely no idea that they were dealing with a force that was similar in size to their own but much better equipped. This was the case regarding both armour and artillery, with a 1:4 and 1:3 ratio respectively.

Believing that a mere 400 Mongolian and Soviet soldiers were facing them east of the Halha River, the Japanese moved their forces during the night of 27/28 May to launch a general attack at dawn. The 3rd Battalion, supported by the artillery, was to launch a series of frontal attacks against the enemy line while the Manchukuoan cavalry was to flank the enemy positions by advancing along the southern side of the Holsten River thus preventing any opposing forces from crossing the river. Crucially, the 23rd Reconnaissance Regiment was to advance on its own and establish a blocking

A destroyed BA-10 armoured car. While heavily armed, these were also very thinly armoured and thus highly vulnerable to even the 7.7mm AT rounds fired by the Japanese Type 92 machine guns. 13 of these vehicles were lost in two days as a result. (Albert Grandolini Collection)

A BA-6 amoured car and its crew. The roughly three dozen such vehicles available during the 28 and 29 May battle proved a decisive advantage for the Soviets and Mongolians, as the Yamagata Detachment had nothing even remotely comparable to these. (Albert Grandolini Collection)

the divisional headquarters was overrun and the unit's CO, Colonel Shoaaiibuu, was killed along with his staff. Nonetheless, the Japanese attack gradually lost momentum. Indeed, it became increasingly difficult to coordinate operations as the closer they moved toward the Halha River, the more they found themselves targeted by accurate artillery fire, as well as by armoured cars. A reliable communications network letting them down as always, by midday, most of the battalion sub-units had stopped any further advance and were busy digging-in around 1,500 metres from the river and still kilometres away from the bridge. The hammer action stopped in its tracks; the anvil became irrelevant. Tragically, the breaking of radio-communications prevented Colonel Yamagata from informing Lieutenant Colonel Azuma of this crucial development.

In the meantime, 57th KON headquarters reacted to these developments by dispatching Colonel Ivenkov, the head of operations of the Corps staff, to coordinate the MPRA and RKKA units engaged in the battle. Together with Colonel Ivenkov went the 149th Motorised Rifle Regiment of the 36th Motorised Rifle Division and several artillery batteries, including one of 122mm howitzers. Similarly, the MPRA rushed elements of the 8th Cavalry Division – including its armoured squadron – to the area. Leaving Tamsag that evening, their first encounter with the enemy occurred the following day.[6]

The Doomed Regiment

During the night of 27/28 May, the 220-strong 23rd Reconnaissance Regiment managed to close on its target without being detected. At dawn, the unit had reached dunes situated a mere 1.7 kilometres away from the bridge when it was sighted by the Soviet reserves. The Japanese soon found themselves under very intensive fire from AT guns, armoured cars and 76mm guns. Effectively, as soon as the enemy came into view, SU-1 battery commander, Senior Lieutenant Vakhtin, took the initiative and ordered his guns to move on the eastern bank of the Halha River. Once in place, they unleashed devastating fire on the Japanese. Following close behind were Bykov's reserves. The consequence was that the 23rd Reconnaissance Regiment – all the while having reached a position where it could fulfil its mission of blocking the retreat of enemy forces – found itself

position near the Soviet-built bridge. The logic of this manoeuvre was that Soviet-Mongolian forces east of the Halha River were then to be trapped between the hammer formed by the 64th Infantry Regiment and the anvil of the 23rd Reconnaissance Regiment. Their only other escape route, across the Holsten River, was to be blocked by the Manchukuoan cavalry. In a typical Japanese way, the operation included no fewer than six distinct axes of advances with four of these stemming from the 3rd Battalion's companies operating independently.

At sunrise the assault began as intended: the Manchukuoan troops made rapid headway along their side of the Holsten River easily chasing away the few small MPRA cavalry detachments, and in the meantime the 3rd Battalion launched its multiple-pronged assault against the MPRA 15th and 17th Cavalry regiments. Benefiting from the effect of surprise, the Japanese infantry columns successfully overwhelmed the two Mongolian units. The MPRA 15th Cavalry was forced to retreat toward the Halha River while the 17th Cavalry Regiment pulled back to the Holsten River. This forced the flanking Soviet motorised companies to follow. During the chaos,

Table 5: Opposing Forces, 28-29 May 1939	
Units	Notes
RKKA & MPRA	CO Colonel Ivenkov, from 29 May
6th Cavalry Division	CO Colonel Shoaaiibuu. 15th and 17th Cavalry Regiments, one training company, one artillery battery and one armoured car squadron
Bykov Detachment	CO Major Bykov. 175th Rifle Machine-Gun Battalion, including eight T-37s, one armoured car squadron (16 BA-6s), one reconnaissance platoon (5 BA-6s and FAI), one SPG battery (4 SU-1s)
149th Motorised Rifle Regiment	CO Major Remisov. Two motorised infantry battalions, reinforced with several artillery batteries
8th Cavalry Division	Units including one armoured squadron
Yamagata Detachment	CO Colonel Yamagata Takemitsu
64th Infantry Regiment HQ	
64th Infantry Regiment Gun Company	3 Type 41 infantry guns, 4 Type 94 AT guns
3rd Infantry Battalion, 64th Infantry Regiment	9th to 12th Infantry companies, one support company with eight HMG and two Type 92 battalion guns
23rd Reconnaissance Regiment	CO Lieutenant Colonel Azuma Yaozo. One tankette company, one cavalry squadron
1st Cavalry Regiment	Hsingan Cavalry Division, nominally 458 men divided into three cavalry and one MG squadrons but understrength (recruited in Inner Mongolia)
7th Cavalry Regiment	Understrength Hsingan Cavalry Division (recruited in Inner Mongolia)
8th Cavalry Regiment	Understrength Hsingan Cavalry Division (recruited in Inner Mongolia)

MPRA troopers of the 6th Cavalry Division. Dispersed in small and widely separated positions, they proved unable to resist the initial onslaught of the IJA's 3rd Battalion on 28 May. (Albert Grandolini Collection)

Lieutenant Colonel Azuma ordered his men to stand firm in the belief that positions must be held at all costs. In the absence of new orders, he was prepared to fight to the last man and the last bullet. Despite subsequent reinforcements, by late evening he had lost 19 men with and 72 wounded. This continued into the night with several enemy attacks having to be repulsed. The following day the Soviets submitted the beleaguered Japanese to even more intense artillery fire from several newly arrived batteries. These included one made up of four 122mm M1910/30 howitzers. Disaster struck at 6.30 in the morning when a shell fragment ruptured the tank of a sedan. The burning fuel soon spread to the truck carrying the regiment's remaining ammunition causing it to explode. This led to other trucks catching fire and the death of several wounded who were using them as shelter.

The day continued with the Soviets launching a series of all-out attacks against Azuma's regiment. The Japanese managed to repulse several of them, however they remained impotent against armoured cars unhindered by return fire from anti-tank weapons. The complete lack of return fire also gave the Soviets the time to dig their own foxholes a few dozen metres away from Japanese positions. The results were seen when Lieutenant Colonel Azuma led 20 surviving men on a *Gyokusai* ('shattered jewel') suicide charge: most were mown down by machine gun fire almost immediately.[7]

A Certain Komdiv Zhukov

The 23rd Reconnaissance

hopelessly tied down. Worse, the MPRA and Soviet units forced to retreat by the 3rd Battalion also arrived on the scene. They engaged the isolated Japanese unit resulting in it being encircled.

By midday, Lieutenant Colonel Azuma had ordered his men to dig foxholes and trenches to protect themselves from the withering enemy artillery fire. However, his men were already short of drinking water and radio contact could not be established with the rest of the detachment. Oblivious to the fact that his mission had failed,

Regiment annihilated, and the 3rd Battalion's sub-units shattered, the Yamagata Detachment was in dire straits. Indeed, after their defeat the Soviets and the Mongolians were now free to target the Japanese with new attacks. Accordingly, the Japanese troops remained on the defensive while reinforcements arrived on the evening of 30 May. They consisted of an infantry company and the MG company of the 2nd Battalion, 71st Infantry Regiment, as well as four Type 94 AT guns and two Type 38 batteries from the

A Soviet officer in front of an abandoned Type 94 Tankette of the 23rd Reconnaissance Regiment. The Japanese lost somewhere between two and 10 of these armoured vehicles on 28 and 29 May. (Albert Grandolini Collection)

RKKA machine gunners in action, firing their M1910 against enemy positions. (Albert Grandolini Collection)

rather unconvincingly, that both sides had won one battle and lost another. Face-saving or not, the 23rd Division had taken a beating: not only was the 23rd Reconnaissance Regiment annihilated but the other units of the Yamagata Detachment had suffered 118 casualties with an unknown number of Manchukuoan losses. The Japanese also lost 10 tankettes, one Type 94 gun, 19 machine guns, six grenade-dischargers, eight trucks and two cars. The Soviets also paid dearly for their victory: 138 men were killed or were missing in action, and another 198 had been wounded with the Bykov Detachment numbering about half of these

13th Field Artillery Regiment. However, these units numbering a total of 366 men, the collective forces were not enough to reverse the situation. Fortunately for Yamagata, their arrival gave the impression of a much larger force with Colonel Ivenkov suspending all offensive operations in the expectation of a Japanese counter-attack. The pause in fighting gave the 3rd Battalion the opportunity to send out search parties from 29 to the 31 May. They were able to retrieve the bodies of their fallen comrades and following a series of inconclusive artillery exchanges on the last day they were able to make an unimpeded withdrawal from the battlefield.

Surprisingly enough, the Soviets did not realise the Japanese had withdrawn until 3 June. It turned out that 23rd Division's HQ demonstrated little interest in escalating the incident and that it was content to consider the May fights as a draw. Indeed, they argued,

casualties. A total of 13 armoured cars (either Soviet or Mongolian) having been lost in the fighting as were 15 vehicles and three guns,[8] the Soviets were less than pleased with their performance.

By mid-May both Stalin and Marshal Kliment Voroshilov, the Commissar for Defence, were expecting the conflict to escalate even though they had doubts about the battle-readiness of the 57th KON. As a result, Komdiv Gueorgui Konstantinovitch Zhukov – then deputy commander of the Belorussian Military District – was summoned to Moscow where he met with Voroshilov. While he was relatively unknown at the time, cavalry officer Zhukov was well acquainted with mechanised warfare and had gained a reputation for being both a disciplinarian and a decisive commander. He was ordered to go to Mongolia to make a thorough assessment of the Special Corps, and after his arrival at the 57th KON's frontline HQ in Tamtsak Bulak on 27 May he was able to head for the battlefield situated 120 kilometres away. After observing the battle between Soviet and Japanese forces he sent his own assessment to Moscow. A damning report, it noted:

> An especially disorganised battle took place on 28 May, led only by the commanders of small units. On 29 May, the enemy occupied several heights 2 to 3 kilometres east of the Khalkhin-Gol and our units attempted to retake them with frontal attacks. At the end of this extremely disorganised combat, our units had lost 71 men with 80 wounded and 33 missing. The reasons for these losses and of these unsatisfactory results are:
>
> 1. Very bad tactical organisation.
>
> 2. Battle leadership was delegated to Colonel Ivenkov (head of Operations Department, Staff 57th KON) who was sent alone and without liaisons.

3. Ignorance of the on-field situation demonstrated by the Corps commander.[9]

He was not incorrect. Soviet units had been thrown piecemeal into the battle while coordination with the artillery proved lacking from beginning to end.

Zhukov's report was backed up by other officers who equally mentioned an endemic disorganisation amongst the 57th KON. This factor eventually doomed Komdiv N.V. Feklenko's prospects of further leading the Corps, and he along with most of his staff were relieved of their duties on 6 June. Zhukov and other officers took their place, with Zhukov's plan being much more ambitious in the long run than simply defending the line that Mongolian-Soviet authorities claimed to be a border.[10]

3

GUNS OF JULY

By that time, Germany had launched the all-out seizure of Czechoslovakia on 15 March 1939. The eruption of a full-scale war in Europe was looking increasingly likely, and in response Moscow was in the middle of negotiating a military alliance with France and Great Britain. It also made openings to Berlin thanks to the efforts of spies such as Richard Sorge. The Soviets became aware that Berlin was reluctant to reinforce further its alliance with Tokyo, and on the back of this Stalin opted to use the Nomonhan incident as an opportunity to teach the Japanese a lesson. This was to dissuade them from restarting war with the USSR, an aspect that was important given the latter's probable commitment to war on its western border. Consequently, Zhukov was ordered to destroy the Japanese forces operating in the contested area between the Halha River and Nomonhan but was ordered not to penetrate uncontested Manchukuoan territory to avoid an escalation into an all-out war. At the same time, he was to reinforce the bridgehead on the eastern bank of the Halha River and be ready to counter-attack decisively in case of a Japanese offensive.

Soviet Preparations

At first, the 57th KON intelligence apparatus was reshuffled, and all the intelligence gathered from the interrogation of prisoners, air reconnaissance and infiltrations into enemy territory were dispatched to a single cell tasked with establishing an overall picture of enemy activities.

On 12 June Zhukov moved the 57th KON's advanced headquarters from Tamats-Bulak towards Hamar-Daba, a mere four kilometres from the bridgehead. On the 19th, the 57th KON was renamed the 1st Army Group, whereas on 5 June, a Front came into being under Komandarm Shtern with authority over the 1st and 2nd Separate Red Bannered Armies, the Trans-Baikal Military District as well as the 57th KON. In essence, these were all the RKKA's forces in the Soviet Far East.

This reorganisation considerably eased the management of a massive shuttle system connecting the Borziya railhead to the Halha

River. Before long, 5,855 mobilised lorries, buses and tankers were shuttling day and night across the 350 kilometres separating the railhead from the frontline, thus providing the 57th KON with the logistical tail it needed to fight a protracted battle. Indeed, once at full pace, the shuttle was able to carry a staggering 56,000 tons of supplies and petrol between 19 July and 31 August 1939. This logistical feat proved decisive throughout the conflict because such an achievement was unthinkable for the Japanese. The latter indeed remained convinced that they held a decisive advantage in terms of lines of communications, and constantly underestimated Soviet strength and capabilities.

From early June, almost the entire Special Corps was concentrated in the vicinity of the contested area. By the end of the month, the bridgehead on the eastern bank of the Halha River was held by the 175th Rifle Machine-Gun Battalion of the 11th Tank Brigade, and positions south of the Holsten River were held by the 149th Motorised Rifle Regiment and the 9th Motor-Mechanised Brigade. These forces were relatively concentrated as the depth of the bridgehead reached roughly five kilometres. Behind them, on the high ground on the western bank of the Halha, the Soviets had positioned three artillery battalions with 12 M1934 152mm and eight M1910/30 122mm howitzers as well as four M1902/30 76mm field guns and 10 M1927 regimental guns. An armoured company of the 8th Motor-Mechanised Brigade was kept in reserve along with 18 armoured cars. Altogether, these units had roughly 3,200 men, 62 armoured cars, 53 machine guns, forty 76mm calibre guns and seven M1932 AT guns. Furthermore, the 6th and the 8th MPRA Cavalry Divisions were also grouped along the western bank of the Halha to cover the flanks of the Soviet pocket against any enemy crossing. The 1st Army Group also kept a powerful mobile reserve 120 kilometres away, at Tamats-Bulak. Here, the 24th Motorised Rifle Regiment, the 7th and 8th Motor-Mechanised Brigades and the 11th Tank Brigade were massed and ready to move to the frontline if needed. By early July, the Soviets had amassed around 12,000 men with 186 tanks and 266 armoured cars in the area to face a new Japanese attack.[1]

Table 6: RKKA-MPRA Order of Battle, 1 July 1939
Units
Eastern shore of the Khalkin Gol (Halha River)
9th Motor-Mechanised Brigade
175th Rifle-Machine-Gun Battalion; 11th Tank Brigade
149th Motorised Rifle Regiment
Western shore of the Khalkin Gol (Halha River)
6th Cavalry Division (MPRA)
8th Cavalry Division (MPRA)
175th Artillery Regiment; 36th Motorised Rifle Division (less one battalion)
3rd Battalion; 185th Artillery Regiment
One armoured car company, 8th Motor-Mechanised Brigade
Operational reserve: Tamats-Bulak or in transit toward the Halha River
24th Motorised Rifle Regiment; 36th Motorised Rifle Division
11th Tank Brigade
7th Motor-Mechanised Brigade
8th Motor-Mechanised Brigade (moving toward Tamats-Bulak)
185th Artillery Regiment (less one battalion)
1st Battalion; 175th Artillery Regiment; 36th Motorised Rifle Division

Japanese Paradoxes

The Japanese remained unconcerned about Soviet activities in the Nomonhan area during the first half of June. Indeed, the Soviet reinforcement of their bridgehead remained largely unnoticed with the Japanese estimating that their presence on the eastern shore of the Halha remained limited to small detachments. Furthermore, the numerous reconnaissance flights flown by the VVS over Manchukuoan territory did not attract any significant reaction from the Japanese either. Indeed, neither the Kwantung Army nor the AGS were eager to cause trouble once the infamous Tientsin Incident began in China. On 14 June 1939, Japanese troops surrounded the British concession in the Chinese city after the British authorities had refused to hand over several Chinese militants suspected of having murdered a Japanese official a few months earlier. This ignited a major diplomatic crisis between London and Tokyo, the two empires looked to be on verge of declaring war on each other. The crisis was however gradually defused and ended with the British handing the suspects over to the Japanese a few weeks later.

The situation changed dramatically on 17 June. That day, VVS aircraft bombed a Manchukuoan outpost and a settlement near Lake Buir, and this bombing was followed by an air strike against the village of Arshaan the next day. On 20 June, it was the turn of a logistical depot in the vicinity of Kanchuerhmiao to be targeted by Soviet aircraft, and in this attack 500 drums of fuel were destroyed along with 380 bags of grain. On 18 and 19 June the Manchukuoan 7th Cavalry Regiment was attacked by a battalion-sized force supported by armoured cars and artillery and had to withdraw as a result.

Once informed of the attacks, on 19 June the Kwantung Army Staff went into a frenzy. Major Tsuji Masanobu played a pivotal role in convincing his colleagues at the Operation Section to launch a massive retaliation, arguing that the failure to do so would only entice the Soviets to encroach further into Manchukuo. Consequently, an operational plan involving an offensive by the entire 7th Division reinforced by a regiment of the 23rd Division and the 1st Tank Group was hastily drafted before being submitted to General Ueda Kenkichi, the Army's Chief of Staff. Kenkichi, however, vetoed the dispatch of the full 7th Division to avoid a loss of face of the 23rd Division's commander. The planning of the operation was reshuffled accordingly giving the main role to the 23rd Division. Meanwhile, the AGS did not object to a divisional-sized sweep to expel RKKA and MPRA forces from the eastern bank of the Halha River provided the intervention remained limited.

The Air Raid Affair

In the skies the situation was also heating up with VVS and IJAAF aircraft engaged in an ever-increasing number of aerial combats. As a result, the Kwantung Army HQ authorised a large-scale air strike targeting the VVS airfields located around Tamsag Bulak in Mongolia with the forthcoming offensive led by 23rd Division in mind. The Kwantung Army Staff deliberately hid this operation from the AGS, the latter, nonetheless, suspected something was in the air. Indeed, it noted in a telegram dated 24 June that:

A Type 95 of the 4th Tank Regiment advances together with soldiers of the 64th Infantry Regiment. (Albert Grandolini Collection)

The 3rd Tank Regiment advances using Type 89 medium tanks advancing in columns. By 1939, these designs, largely inspired from the French FT-17, were obsolete. (Albert Grandolini Collection)

The policy of the Amy General Staff is to prevent the border conflict from spreading. During operations to repel enemy forces invading Manchukuoan territory in the west, it is essential that maximum efforts be made to avoid any fighting on other border fronts, and that no air attacks be mounted against Outer Mongolian territory to the west. It is believed that this policy accords with that of the Kwantung Army. In particular, the bombing of Outer Mongolian territory is considered improper, as it will lead to the gradual extension of bombing assaults by both sides behind the opposing frontiers, thus prolonging the incident.[2]

The telegram failed to impress the *Gekokujo*-minded Kwantung Army, the air raid was not only maintained, but it was also conducted ahead of the initial planning to pre-empt the arrival of an AGS envoy. On 27 June, early in the morning, the IJAAF attacked several VVS air bases, claiming to have destroyed dozens of aircraft in the process.[3] This did not go down well with the AGS which expressed its displeasure as such: "[The AGS] fundamentally disagrees with your policy and it is sincerely regretted that advanced notice of your intent was not received. Needless to say, this matter has such far-reaching consequences that it can by no means be left to your unilateral decision. Hereafter existing policy will be definitely and strictly observed".[4]

Incensed by what was perceived as AGS meddling into their jurisdiction, the Kwantung Army Staff (but more probably Major Tsuji Masanobu acting alone) shot back with another telegram stating that: "There appear to be certain differences between Army General Staff and this Army in evaluating the battlefield situation and the measures that need to be adopted. It is requested that the handling of trivial matters in border areas be entrusted to this Army".[5]

This reply being enough to tip the balance, on 29 June the Imperial General Headquarters replied with a direct and mandatory order defining precisely what the Kwantung Army was allowed to do in the foreseeable future, thus defining Japanese stance during the rest of the Nomonhan Incident:

Directives:
a) It is the responsibility of the Kwantung Army to localise matters in the settlement of border disputes.

b) Areas in which the border is disputed, or in which defence is tactically unfeasible, need not be defended.

Orders:
c) Ground combat will be limited to the border region between Manchukuo and Outer Mongolia east of Lake Buir Nor.
d) Enemy bases will not be attacked from the air.[6]

The Build-up of IJA Forces
Accordingly, the Japanese build-up in the Nomonhan area began with the arrival of a vanguard of the 23rd Division at Chiangchunmiao on 22 June while two days later a Japanese detachment was attacked by a Soviet company-sized force supported by armour. Six Japanese soldiers were killed and another 20 were wounded in the encounter, whereas on the Soviet side seven were killed and at least four vehicles were left behind following their withdrawal. By the end of the month, the build-up at Chiangchunmiao had been completed with the arrival of elements of the 7th Division, foremost the 26th Infantry Regiment. This unit had been motorised for the occasion by linking it up with the 3rd Motorised Transport Regiment as well as two anti-tank and two field artillery companies. Additionally, the Kwantung Army sent all its bridging equipment. Because of the endemic lack of trucks, the bulk of the 23rd Division infantry regiments had to make the 200-kilometre journey from Hailar to Chiangchunmiao on foot.

Another powerful force, the Yasukoa Detachment, was concentrated in Arshaan. This was based on Lieutenant General Yasukoa Masamo's 1st Tank Group which controlled the 3rd, and the 4th Tank Regiments, i.e., virtually the entire tank inventory available in Manchuria. The 3rd Tank Regiment under Colonel Yoshimaru Kiyotake had 26 Type 89, four brand-new Type 97 medium tanks as well as 11 Type 94 and Type 97 tankettes, while the 4th Tank Regiment under Colonel Tamada Yoshio, had 35 Type 95 Ha-Go light tanks, eight Type 89 medium tanks and three Type 94 tankettes. Joining these forces were the 2nd Battalion of the 7th Division's 28th Infantry Regiment, the 24th Engineer Regiment and the 1st Independent Field Artillery Regiment equipped with eight Type 90 field guns.

In all, the Kwantung Army concentrated 13 infantry battalions supported by roughly 70 tanks and 68 field or mountain guns (15,000 men in total) to destroy the Soviet bridgehead. This was

Table 7: Japanese Order of Battle; 1 July 1939	
Units	**Notes**
23rd Division	CO Lieutenant General Komatsubara Michitaro
Left (western) shore force	CO Major General Kobayashi Koichi
71st Infantry Regiment	CO Colonel Okamoto Tokuzo
72nd Infantry Regiment	CO Colonel Sakai Mikio
26th Infantry Regiment	CO Colonel Sumi Shinichiro. Motorised and to be used as a support force
23rd Engineer Regiment	CO Lieutenant Colonel Saito Isamu
1st Independent Field Artillery Regiment	CO Colonel Miyao Kan. Two batteries with four Type 90 75mm field guns each
13th Field Artillery Regiment	CO Colonel Ise Takahide. 1st and 3rd Battalions. 16 Type 38 75mm field guns and eight Type 38 120mm Field Howitzers
23rd Reconnaissance Regiment	CO Lieutenant Colonel Ioki Eiichi. Badly understrength, tasked with securing the bridge. Reinforced with a company of the 64th Infantry Regiment
3rd Battalion, 64th Infantry Regiment	Kept as a reserve
Yasuoka Detachment	CO Lieutenant General Yasuoka Masaomi
3rd Tank Regiment	CO Colonel Yoshimaru Kiyotake. 30 medium tanks, 11 tankettes
4th Tank Regiment	CO Colonel Tamada Yoshio. 35 light tanks, eight medium tanks, three tankettes
64th Infantry Regiment	CO Colonel Yamagata Takemitsu. 1st and 2nd Battalions
24th Engineer Regiment	
2nd Battalion, 13th Field Artillery Regiment	Eight Type 38 75mm field guns and four Type 38 120mm Field Howitzers
2nd Battalion, 28th Infantry Regiment	CO Major Kajikawa Tomiji
Hsingan Cavalry Division	Kept as a reserve and for rear and flank security duties. 1st, 4th, 5th, 7th, 8th, 12th Cavalry Regiments

attacks. However, two essential aspects were to influence the implementation of the entire Japanese plan: there was only enough bridging equipment to assemble a single bridge spanning a maximum of 80 metres; the pontoons used in the operation dated from the Russo-Japanese War and, therefore, could not endure the carrying of heavy vehicles such as tanks. The Halha River was swelled by the rains and there were few places where its width was inferior to 80 metres. This left only a few places where the river's width was less than 80 metres, the Japanese 23rd Engineer Regiment had no other choice but to select a crossing site roughly 20 kilometres north of the Soviet bridges between the Fui Height on the eastern shore and the Bain Tsagan Height on the western shore. This being despite the banks reaching a height of 30 meters. Correspondingly, the Japanese had to use their tanks – unable to cross the Halha River – to make their frontal assaults against the Soviet pocket while it was their infantry alone that were to cross the Halha and conduct the envelopment

expected to be more than enough as the enemy forces defending the latter were estimated at 1,000 men supported by a dozen guns and several dozen armoured vehicles. Even more so, on the eve of the offensive Japanese reconnaissance aircraft spotted several Soviet trucks leaving the area. Overlooking the fact that these were simply the vehicles involved in the logistical shuttle supplying the 1st Army Group and returning empty to the rear depots, the Japanese concluded that the enemy was withdrawing. Apart from faulty intelligence of this kind, there were other crucial flaws in the Japanese endeavour: the Yasukoa Detachment was not a well-honed mechanised combined arms grouping but an ad-hoc assembly of various forces not used to operating together, and the Japanese possessed only 28 Type 94 anti-tank guns. To make up for this lack of anti-tank capability, the Japanese had to improvise their own version of the Molotov Cocktail by filling glass bottles with a mix of sand and gasoline before plugging them with a piece of cotton.[7]

Initially drawn up by Major Tsuji, the operational plan for the forthcoming offensive was a "hammer and anvil" concept typical to the IJA. A main force was to cross the Halha River by surprise, it was to follow the western bank, then it was to attack the rear of the Soviet bridgehead on the eastern shore and destroy their bridges located near the confluence between the Halha and the Holsten rivers.

In the meantime, a second force was to keep the RKKA units defending these bridges busy by launching a series of frontal manoeuvre that was to seal the enemy's fate.

Accordingly, Lieutenant General Komatsubura Michitaro organised his forces into two main components. The task of crossing the Halha River was handed to Major General Kobayashi Koichi who led the 71st and 72nd Infantry Regiment while the 26th Infantry Regiment was to be used as a supporting force once the Japanese had crossed. Next, the 3rd Battalion of the 64th Infantry Regiment was to be kept in reserve while the 13th Field Artillery and 1st Independent Field Artillery Regiments were to provide artillery support. Because of the limitations linked to the bridge, only one battalion of the former regiment would be dispatched on the western shore of the river. Altogether, Kobayashi had roughly 8,000 men at his disposal. The second force, the Yosuoka Detachment, was reinforced with the remaining two battalions of the 64th Infantry Regiment and one battalion of the 13th Field Artillery Regiment. This was to compensate for the loss of the 1st Independent Field Artillery Regiment which had been re-assigned to the first force.[8]

The Crossing

Lieutenant General Komatsubara launched his general offensive very early on 1 July. The 71st Infantry Regiment, followed by the 72nd Infantry Regiment, began its advance toward the Fui Height which it reached in the evening. The only resistance met by the Japanese that day was a few armoured cars which fired on the advancing infantry

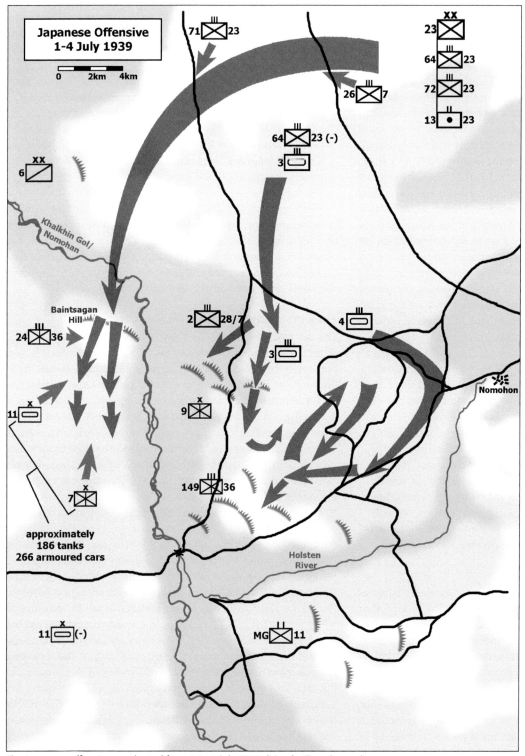

The Japanese offensive conducted from 1 to 4 July 1939. (Map by Tom Cooper)

across the Halha River. The battalion met no resistance and captured the Bain Tsagan Heights on the western shore during the night. In the meantime troops of the 23rd Engineer Regiment rushed to assemble the pontoon bridge. On the other hand, they encountered countless difficulties such as the sandy soil. It severely complicated the task of anchoring of the bridge while the steep banks made the carrying of the pontoons' sub-elements exhausting work.

The bridge was only completed at 0630, a time much later than expected, meanwhile the other battalions of the 71st Infantry Regiment and the 72nd Infantry Regiments used the boats which were shuttling across the river so as not to waste further time. Several of the 18 Type 94 AT guns, twelve 75mm field guns and four 120mm howitzers carried by the Japanese on the western shore also had to be disassembled and reassembled to be brought across the river by boat.

The bridge soon also proved to be somewhat of a bottleneck for Colonel Sumi's 26th Infantry Regiment. Not only did the trucks have to be emptied before crossing the bridge and then reloaded, but only one vehicle could cross at a time. Accordingly, it was only at noon on 3 July that the first of its three battalions had regrouped on the western bank. Out of desperation, Colonel Sumi ordered his two remaining battalions to leave their trucks on the eastern shore and deploy as foot infantry. The consequence of this was that the Japanese just lost their motorised support force that had been expected to dash towards the rear of the enemy bridgehead.

Meanwhile, also at dawn, the 71st Infantry Regiment had been attacked by the Mongolian 15th Cavalry Regiment supported by several armoured cars. However, this was easily repulsed once the first Type 94 AT guns arrived on the scene and two vehicles that had penetrated the Japanese line were destroyed. Soon, the 71st and the 72nd Infantry Regiments began to advance toward the Komatsu Heights seven kilometres away. Once the latter was taken, the Japanese would make the last 10-kilometre leg towards the enemy bridges. So far, and apart from the loss of time and confusion caused

from a distance, and they continued until they were forced away by artillery fire losing two vehicles in the process. One Japanese soldier was killed and another four were wounded during the engagement. The following day, one of the Japanese battalions lost its way while attempting to rally on the Fui Heights. Indeed, these 'heights' were nothing more than a 10-metre-high plateau and were, therefore, easy to miss. In another incident, one company found itself straddled along the Halha's eastern bank, roughly six kilometres north-east of the Fui Heights. Here, it encountered enemy machine guns and artillery located on the other side of the river. Twenty-four soldiers were killed.

This however acted as a diversion that hid the main concentration of Japanese forces. In the evening, 71st Infantry Regiment was sent by the deficient bridging equipment, the main Japanese thrust had gone almost flawlessly.[9]

Yasuoka's Night Attack

While these events were taking place at 4 a.m. on 2 July, the Yasuoka Detachment moved from the area around Chiangchunmiao with the orders to launch a dawn attack against the bridgehead. By the end of the afternoon, however, its CO received a new set of intelligence stating that airmen had reportedly sighted the Soviets withdrawing from their positions on the eastern shore. As a result, Lieutenant General Yasuoka Masaomi decided to launch an all-out pursuit operation in the evening without consulting with Lieutenant General Komatsubara Michitaro and even though Japanese tank doctrine did not contain information relating to full-scale regimental tank assaults at night. There being next to no intelligence on the number of enemy forces, and only information on the position of their three defensive lines, the order created some turmoil among the 4th Tank Regiment with several officers opposing the plan to attack at night. This was until Colonel Tamada Yoshio set the record straight by issuing the following order, and all the while explicitly acknowledging the validity of the objections raised:

It is regrettable that the regiment did not break through enemy lines during the daylight hours, but the mission cannot be delayed. If we let things ride, this would remain a blot on history for many years to come. If we carry out a determined advance at night, there is still hope of breaking through. Consequently, from now the regiment will seek and destroy the foe wherever he is encountered while advancing toward the confluence. It seems foolhardy to commit a large tank unit to battle at night without knowledge of the enemy's position and the terrain. Nonetheless, these are the requirements of the mission and I therefore earnestly request that all officers and men act as one to centre on the unit commander. For the honour of the regiment, we push forward facing the risk of annihilation.[10]

And so it was that the 3rd and 4th Tank Regiments launched their unsupported attacks during the evening. The first problem that came to light was that Japanese tank personnel having served in China had become used to advancing without giving much thought to coordinating with the infantry. A second was that the 64th Infantry Regiment had been hopelessly delayed after finding itself on the receiving end of a two-hour-long Soviet artillery barrage. Next, 13th Field Artillery Regiment failed to make any impression. This was perhaps due to its having been seconded to the Yasuoka Detachment virtually at the last minute, to make up for the reassignment of the 1st Independent Field Artillery Regiment to support the crossing of the bulk of the 23rd Division. Foremost, Japanese gunners proved reluctant to move their guns too far ahead because of the limited range of their weapons and the vulnerability of their horses to Soviet counterbattery fire.

Surprisingly enough, the two tank regiments escaped largely unscathed. This was despite rapidly losing their cohesiveness once the fighting started and their carrying out assaults at different times. The 3rd attacked at 2000 hours and the 4th two hours later with a fierce thunderstorm erupting around midnight. The assault stunned the Soviets, and Japanese tanks easily broke through the lines of the 9th Motor-Mechanised Brigade and of the 149th Rifle Regiment. Elements of the 4th Tank Regiment destroyed enemy artillery batteries and claimed to have destroyed a dozen enemy guns, but both units met with increasing resistance once they

reached the Soviet third line and were targeted by heavy artillery and antitank fire. According to Colonel Tamada, the Japanese were also confronted with insurmountable command and control difficulties:

Among the things from which I suffered most as commander was insufficient communication and uncertainty about positions. There being absolutely no communication facilities between us and higher headquarters or neighbouring units, contact had to depend on messengers. Despite wide-open terrain, there were no distinctive landmarks in the area, so it was extremely difficult to perceive locations or to find units.[11]

Wisely enough, both regiment commanders ordered their troops to withdraw before dawn. Though it had failed to come anywhere near destroying the bridgehead, the Yasuoka Detachment did succeed in sowing panic among the Soviets while suffering from very limited losses. Indeed, only one man from the 4th Tank Regiment was killed while seven others were wounded.[12]

Zhukov's Gamble

The air raid of 27 June had two contradictory effects. Firstly, reconnaissance missions flown by the VVS decreased markedly, and the Soviets were unable to detect Japanese concentrations before the beginning on the offensive. Secondly, the raid gave warning that the Japanese were making plans and it was thought that it may involve a renewed ground offensive against their bridgehead. Not taking any chances and seeking to have a powerful counter-attack force on hand if needed, Zhukov ordered the 7th Motor-Mechanised Brigade, the 11th Tank Brigade and the 24th Motorised Rifle Regiment to leave Tamsag Bulak and move toward the front. The three units departed during the night of 1/2 July, and they were well underway when the Yasuoka Detachment struck the bridgehead sowing much confusion on the process.

Still ignoring that the bulk of the 23rd Division had crossed the Halha River, Zhukov ordered them to group near the bridgehead before crossing, then to launch a massive counter-attack on the flanks of the Yasuoka Detachment. By dawn on 3 July, however, the MPRA 15th Cavalry Regiment signalled at last the presence of strong enemy forces at Bain Tsagan. The Soviet commander reacted by diverting the still advancing reinforcements and launching an all-out and multi-pronged assault against Bain Tsagan. The armoured component of the 6th Cavalry Division, reinforced by a battalion of the 11th Tank Brigade, was to attack head-on, while the rest of the 11th Tank Brigade, the 24th Motorised Rifle Regiment and the 7th Motor-Mechanised Brigades were to do so from the north, northwest and south respectively. Nevertheless, time dictated that this complex manoeuvre could not be carried out in a well-coordinated fashion. In essence, it meant that most of these units – still exhausted by their journey from Tamsag Bulak – were to take on the Japanese without having had respite. This led to a series of all-out and uncoordinated charges led by the 11th Tank Brigade.[13] For Zhukov it was clear that the Japanese advance on the western shore of the Halha River had to be stopped at all costs if the bridgehead was to be saved:

At Bain Tsagan, the situation was the following. The infantry was late, and we had only a few second echelon units. There was a real threat that they would force us to give up the bridgehead beyond the Khalkin-Go and our hopes lied on this bridgehead. Under no circumstances was this to be allowed. I took the decision to attack the Japanese with the Yakovlev tank brigade (the 11th Tank Brigade) knowing that it would suffer from heavy losses. However,

A Soviet tank crew just after their surrender to an IJA officer. (Albert Grandolini Collection)

A destroyed BA-6 armoured car. Whereas it had the firepower of a tank, these thinly armoured vehicles were very vulnerable to AT weapons. (Albert Grandolini Collection)

A crew of the 3rd Tank Regiment eating a meal. In the background is one of the unit's four Type 97 medium tanks. (Albert Grandolini Collection)

I took the decision conscientiously. The brigade was around 200 tanks-strong, it deployed and left. The Japanese artillery hurt it very badly but, I repeat, we were ready for it. [...] When I learned that the Japanese had crossed the river, I ordered the Yakovlev brigade to attack. They had another 60-70 kilometres to cross, and they entered directly into the fire of the battle.[14]

The Bain Tsagan Melee

At mid-morning on 3 July, the 11th Tank Brigade launched a two-pronged attack directly after its 60-kilometre approach march from the north-west and west. It collided with the 71st and 72nd Infantry Regiments as these closed on Komatsu Heights. The Soviet charge was chaotic, with the tanks grouped in formations of varying sizes advancing at full speed. The Japanese had a total of 16 Type 94 37mm anti-tank guns, 12 field guns and nine regimental guns, both types being of 75mm calibre, and this armament and weaponry was spread out among three regiments situated on the western bank of the Halha River. When in range of the tanks, they began to attack with devastating effect as even the Type 94 could pierce the BT-5 tank's frontal armour at medium range. Consequently, range was kept to around 400 metres so as not to waste limited amounts of ammunition. The enthusiastic gunners claimed to have destroyed enormous amounts of enemy vehicles. A single battery of three Type 38 field guns reported that it had destroyed a full company of 15 Soviet tanks in 20 minutes in the end of the morning. This was not enough to stop the enemy in its tracks and number of tanks reached the Japanese infantry. Crucially, the Soviet tank crews were trained to concentrate on firing against enemy heavy weapons with their own guns, neglecting the infantry in the process. This made them highly vulnerable to the Japanese *nikuhaku kogeki* (human bullets assaults), infantrymen closed in on the tanks before attacking them with Molotov cocktails or satchel charges. Sometimes, they even climbed on to the tanks' turrets and threw grenades through the hatches.

The Japanese version of the Molotov cocktail proved particularly deadly: the BT tanks not only had gasoline engines, but because they had travelled far at high speed in scorching heat (the temperatures were as high as 38 degrees Celsius that day) they overheated. So, even when Japanese soldiers failed to light the cotton plugging the bottles, their contents burst into flames on contacting the tank's armour plating.

By midday, the 11th Tank Brigade had been decimated and its charge broken. However, they had forced the Japanese to stop their advance as shown by the testimony of a captured Japanese soldier. Written in his diary, it provides a short, but telling glimpse into the chaotic conditions that prevailed that morning: "Several scores of tanks attacked unexpectedly, causing chaos among our troops. Horses stampeded, neighing, and dragging gun carriages with them; cars scattered in all directions. [...] The morale of our troops fell extremely low."[15]

Around midday, it was the turn of the 24th Motorised Rifle Regiment to enter the fray. The unit attacked from the west after a delay caused by a misdirection, but it was too late to support the tanks of the 11th Brigade that had advanced along the same axis a few hours earlier. The 7th Motor-Mechanised brigade arriving on the scene at around 1500 hours, its armoured cars, acting very much as tanks, rushed toward the Japanese positions: dozens of vehicles were lost as they attempted to tie down enemy forces.

As for these Japanese forces they were also experiencing a good number of difficulties. The infantry began to run low on water and there was a shortage of AT ammunition. Finally, a last and better coordinated, three-pronged assault was launched early in the evening but this, too, was repulsed although giving the Soviets victory. For them, the crisis was over, and as the Japanese western offensive had been stopped dead although at a heavy price with dozens of burning armoured vehicles dotting the battlefield.[16]

At a meeting that evening, Lieutenant General Komatsubara, his deputy, Major Tsuji and other officers, concluded that a withdrawal from the western bank was unavoidable. This was due mainly to their bridgehead consisting of a single bridge, and the fact that if it was destroyed their forces would be cut off from the rear. The threat that it could be destroyed had been made abundantly clear by the bombing of a pontoon by the VVS. Though the pontoon had not suffered any damage, the 71st and 72nd Infantry regiments began their withdrawal that night while the 26th Infantry Regiment remained as a covering force on Bain Tsagan.

It was left to resist a series of fierce Soviet attacks throughout 4 July and suffered heavy casualties in the process. This was due mostly to its 1st Battalion finding itself surrounded and threatened with annihilation. In the meantime, Soviet long-range artillery pounded the Japanese troops on the Fui Height throughout the day. Finally, and after having rescued the remnants of the 1st Battalion, the whole regiment withdrew over the following night while the engineers blew up the bridge. Tragically, several soldiers and wounded remained stranded on the western shore and several drowned in their desperate attempt to swim across the Halha River.

One of the IJA Type 89s demolished during the assaults of the 3rd and 4th Tank Regiments against the Soviet bridgehead. (Albert Grandolini Collection)

A Type 94 37mm AT gun in battery. Such weapons proved decisive in decimating the Soviet 11th Tank Brigade on 3 July 1939. (Albert Grandolini Collection)

Whereas the Japanese invoked face-saving arguments such as the efficiency of their anti-tank gunnery during the battle, they had nonetheless suffered another major defeat. Their offensive had not only been repulsed, but losses were also heavy. Effectively, a total of 220 soldiers were killed or missing in action and another 451 were wounded representing a casualty rate of 10 percent, including 278 in the 26th Regiment alone. The success of the Soviet counter-offensive had also come at a heavy price. The 11th Tank Brigade lost 72 out of the 127 BT-5 Tanks committed to the battle as well as half of its ten KhT-26 flamethrower tanks. Thirty-seven of the 59 BA armoured cars committed by the Soviets – mostly from the 7th Motor-Mechanised Brigade – had been lost, the 6th Cavalry Division's armoured battalion lost eight armoured cars, and in total 122 armoured vehicles were lost in one day. A positive point was that, with the Soviets controlling the battlefield, a number of these vehicles could be repaired. As for the 24th Motorised Rifle Regiment, it lost 68 men with 128 wounded over the two days.[17]

Crucially, the Soviets proved fast learners and managed to adapt their battle tactics to reduce their tank casualties. This adaptation was made to mitigate the effects of the enemy Molotov cocktails which had proved so effective on 3 July. Colonel Sumi Shinichiro,

the CO of the 26th Infantry Regiment, gave a detailed assessment of Japanese infantry anti-tank tactics and how the Soviets reacted:

Our equipment was overwhelmingly inadequate, and my regiment had only the following firepower: 6 heavy machine guns, 6 battalion guns, and 2 battalion trench mortars. We had *kampan* (satchel charges) as anti-tank defences, but they were largely ineffective. In the light of the experience gained during the first phase of the Nomonhan Incident, we prepared Molotov cocktails by filling soft-drink and beer bottles with gasoline and capping them with fuses – a new improvisation from the Japanese Army. [...]

We were being subjected to fierce attacks by a group of about 300 enemy tanks. The range was 800 meters, and our infantry guns could score an effective hit only once in three shots. Enemy tanks were able to approach before we could get off more than a few rounds, and we lacked the time to continue firing. The 300 enemy medium tanks roared down upon us and overran our defences, [...] My men frantically hurled Molotov cocktails at the tanks with deadly accuracy. Tanks burst into flame like matchboxes. I counted 84 knocked out enemy tanks. This was the first and last success we ever obtained during the Nomonhan Incident.

On 5 July, the enemy tanks (which had suffered such great losses from our Molotov cocktails) ceased to advance. Instead, they fired randomly at long range, with their hulls buried in the sand, and only their turrets protruding. We sustained heavy casualties from this shelling, as we had no adequate weapons with which to return the fire. About one-third of my men were soon killed or wounded. On 5 July, we commenced to pull back into Manchurian territory. [...]

There is no doubt that the Molotov cocktails were successfully used at the beginning, but their effectiveness dwindled thereafter. The original successes were due, I believe, to the fact that the enemy tank engines were overheated from long and rapid movement in the burning sun. The enemy later screened his tanks with wire-netting to shield them against the Molotov cocktails. Soon afterwards, however, the enemy introduced new medium tanks without wire-netting; the latest tanks did not catch fire as easily as they had during the first encounters.

Finding that Molotov cocktails were now of no avail, our brave soldiers clung to the turrets of enemy tanks, but it was like flies trying to bite a tortoise. Many times, I saw tanks throw off our men by revolving the turrets at high speed. The steel plate on the tanks was too thick for our grenades to be effective. Once assaulted, we had no other alternative than to resist as best we could and then hide in our foxhole, a situation which was not peculiar to my regiment alone.[18]

Piano Wires

The 3 July 1939 turned out to be an inauspicious day for IJA tank crews. The Yasuoka Detachment resumed its offensive against the Soviet bridgehead presuming that the Soviets would be at the end of their tether and had begun to withdraw. The 4th Tank Regiment moved first at around 1000 hours, but before long it was facing a series of counterattacks led by the 9th Motor-Mechanised Brigade combining infantry and armoured cars. Around noon, the Japanese had to counter another flanking attack from the eight BT-5 tanks present in the pocket, while in the afternoon, having claimed to have destroyed several vehicles, Colonel Tamada called off the assault and

Type 95 Ha-Go tanks during one of the 4th Tank Regiment's forays against the Soviet bridgehead. (Albert Grandolini Collection)

One of the Type 92 105mm guns operated by the 7th Heavy Field Artillery Regiment on 23 July 1939. (Albert Grandolini Collection)

Japanese gunners proudly posing with a shell. In the end, the attempt to destroy the Soviet pocket by combining artillery and infantry assaults turned out to be a dismal failure. (Albert Grandolini Collection)

shielded his tanks behind sand dunes. Things got much worst for the 3rd Regiment. It launched an assault around midday along with the 64th Infantry Regiment which, over the previous days, had been badly shaken by the fierce enemy artillery bombardments.

At first, the advancing Japanese easily overwhelmed several Soviet outposts as the undulating terrain protected them from long-range anti-tank gun fire. However, once they pursued toward a series of enemy strong points, the tanks met with something entirely unexpected. To counter any attack, the Soviets had covered whole fields with an almost invisible network of iron wires. They formed dense webs placed along the main approaches to their positions, and they proved to be efficient in slowing down advancing infantry as well as providing an obstacle for tanks. Once tanks had entered the webs, the wires became tangled in the drive-wheels stopping the vehicles stone-dead in their tracks. This left them open to attack from well-entrenched and camouflaged anti-tank guns as well as armoured cars in hull-down positions some 700 to 800 metres away. This turned into a protracted long-range duel between the Japanese medium tanks and the Soviet AT guns and BA armoured cars, with the Japanese having a massive disadvantage.

The Type 89 and the Type 97 medium tanks were armed with a 57mm low-velocity gun intended foremost to fire explosive shells against entrenchments or infantry, and the Soviet 45mm calibre anti-tank and armoured car guns having a much higher velocity and a longer effective range against armoured targets. Not surprisingly the Japanese tanks were knocked out in succession over the next few hours. To make matters worse, tank corps regulations proscribed the abandonment of tanks by their crew while in action and they shared the same fate as their vehicles. It was only at 1900 hours that the 3rd Regiment and the 64th Infantry Regiment were ordered to withdraw. The 64th had been pinned down by enemy fire and had thus been unable to provide any effective support to the tanks.

By evening, the 3rd Tank Regiment was a spent force: 10 of the twenty-one Type 89s engaging at midday had been knocked out as was a single Type 97; and to round things off the highly vulnerable tankettes had not faired any better. As for human casualties, the regiment lost 15 men including its CO Colonel Yoshimaru plus 15 wounded. On 4 July, the 4th Tank Regiment tried its luck once more. However, it proved as pointless as the previous attacks as the advance was instantly stalled by a series of Soviet counterattacks combining armour and infantry, with the fighting going on well into the evening. A similar scenario occurred on 5 July.[19]

The Game of "Two Steps Forward One Step Back"

In the aftermath of the failure at Halha River, Lieutenant General Komatsubara ordered the bulk of his division to concentrate around the Soviet bridgehead and to destroy it by launching all-out frontal attacks. At this stage, Japanese underestimation of the Soviet logistical capabilities and their overestimation of the losses they inflicted became crucial: they believed that the 1st Army Group could not field more than two divisions at the same time; and they also believed that the enemy forces in the area had already been decimated during the previous fighting. Accordingly, it was

thought that one last large effort was all that was needed to put an end to the incident. The Japanese were, by now, well-aware of the major trump cards held by the Soviets. Their control of the heights west of the Halha River gave them a full view of the battlefield, and this allowed them to use to their much superior artillery to its full force; especially as at this stage as their artillerymen had carefully mapped the area and set plenty of markers to aid the use of pre-coordinated fire. Furthermore, the combats of early July had shown that armoured counterattacks could stall any advance at short notice and that Japanese tanks were unable to break through the enemy web of strongpoints. The 23rd Division's officers therefore opted to use their main asset – the Japanese infantrymen training in night and close combat – against what they perceived as the Soviet's main weakness: the inability of their riflemen to do the same. In a sense, this was exactly what the IJA tactical doctrine was all about: the use of martial skills and fighting spirit to win against superior firepower under the cover of darkness. Thus, an all-out night offensive was to allow the 23rd Division to pierce through Soviet lines, targeting the confluence between and the Halha and Holsten rivers to blow up the seven to nine Soviet bridges crossing the Halha, thus sealing the fate of the bridgehead.

As limited daytime attacks continued to be launched with the support of the 4th Tank Regiment, the 64th, 72nd and 26th infantry regiments were redeployed to the northern side of the Holsten River. The 26th acting as a reserve, the 71st Infantry Regiment was deployed to the southern banks of the river to beef-up the Hsingan Cavalry Division, a unit that had shown time and again its inability to cope with Soviet armoured forays. The 28th Infantry Regiment was transferred to Fui Heights where it was to act as a reserve and protect the flanks of the division. At 2130 hours on 7 July, the attack began with a 30-minute artillery barrage as the 64th and 72nd rushed the enemy lines. At first, the Japanese assaults proved highly successful, and their infantry succeeded in infiltrating enemy strongpoints and creating massive confusion. With several Soviet companies firing at each other, the 149th Rifle Regiment fell into disarray and retreated in disorder, its CO Major Remisov being killed in action. If things looked to be going well, the 64th Regiment found itself facing stiff resistance once it had reached Point 733, a position located in the vicinity of the confluence and three kilometres from the Halha River. Perhaps the strongest Soviet strong point of all, it took the unit hours to overwhelm it. The same night, two Japanese parties comprising a few dozen sappers and infantrymen each managed to infiltrate the lines of enemy forces before each blowing

A Type 92 field gun firing on Soviet artillery positions on 24 July 1939. (Albert Grandolini Collection)

up a pontoon bridge. By dawn, nevertheless, the two regiments had failed to break through the confluence. The 64th had to fall back toward its starting position and in the process gave up Point 733, soon to be renamed 'Remisov Heights' by the Soviets. The commander of the 72nd had to order the bulk of his regiment to withdraw out of direct sight from the Soviet artillery, leaving only a single company to hold the positions conquered during the night. While this was taking place, the 71st Infantry Regiment had launched its own assault on the southern bank of the Holsten, targeting the so-called Noro Heights, a small hill overlooking the confluence. By mistake, it seized another hill some six kilometres from its objective.

A company of BT-5s belonging to the 11th Tank Brigade. (Albert Grandolini Collection)

Despite being only partly successful, the offensive shocked the Soviets who rushed reinforcements to the bridgehead on 8 July. As well as the 24th Motorised Rifle Regiment and the 7th Motor-Mechanised Brigade, these forces included the 5th Rifle-Machine Gun Brigade and the 603rd Rifle Regiment, from the 82nd Rifle Division, a unit that had just been transferred from the Soviet Union, and which was deployed to the front-line right upon its arrival. These different units allowed the Soviets to build a much denser defensive system and thus severely complicate Japanese night sorties. Furthermore, RKKA soldiers became familiar with night combat and less prone to panic. The 23rd Division launched other, smaller scale, attacks during the following nights but failed to alter the overall situation. Namely, their infantry usually made significant advances during the night, but had to withdraw at dawn to avoid being plastered by Soviet artillery, leaving only small forces on the conquered positions. During the day, the Soviets used their artillery to pound these advanced detachments before launching counterattacks with a mix of armour and infantry, and invariably succeeded into retaking a part of the lost ground.

A larger-scale attack occurred in the evening of the 11 July, when the 64th Infantry Regiment, reinforced by elements of the 72nd Infantry Regiment attacked Point 733, and succeeded in taking it. This happened after the defending 603rd Rifle Regiment had been deployed to the point after an exhausting 300-kilometre march, and while 20 percent of the unit was made up by raw, barely trained recruits. This left the unit especially vulnerable to the Japanese infantry's mastery of infiltration tactics.

By 0430 hours on 12 July, one of the Japanese battalions had come within 1,500 metres of the river. Before long, the Soviets launched a counter-attack with the 11th Tank Brigade joined by its dreaded flamethrower tank company and supported by riflemen drawn from other units. These forces succeeded in almost cutting off the 1st Battalion from the rest of the 64th Infantry Regiment and they forced the Japanese to give away captured positions at the conclusion of a particularly fierce battle. The 11th Tank Brigade did, however, lose its CO, who was killed by a sniper.

At that point, the Japanese had exhausted themselves, and had suffered 2,122 casualties since 1 July. The 64th and the 72nd Infantry Regiments had lost roughly one-third and one-fifth of their strength respectively between 7 and 12 July, while on 9 July the decimated 1st Tank Group had been ordered back to its garrison, thus ending Japanese armour deployment during the Nomonhan Incident. The artillery and support units had suffered too: 18 field guns had been destroyed and 500 horses killed. On 12 July, the 23rd Division commander ordered a halt of the night offensives and its units to withdraw toward their 6 July position. He concluded that any new similar attempt against the bridgehead would be pointless if the

Another view of the tanks of the 11th Tank Brigade. Despite heavy losses, these succeeded in repulsing the 23rd Division's foray on the western shore of the Halha River. (Albert Grandolini Collection)

A RKKA squad waiting to face the advance of Japanese infantry on 23 July 1939. (Albert Grandolini Collection)

A crew from the 11th Tank Brigade inspecting a captured Japanese Type 11 LMG. (Albert Grandolini Collection)

Machine gunners with M1910 MGs engaging approaching enemy infantry from one of the Soviet strongpoints. (Albert Grandolini Collection)

enemy artillery positioned on the western bank of the Halha River had not been neutralised beforehand.[20]

The Big Guns

The dispatch of heavy artillery from Japan toward the Kwantung Army had already been scheduled by the AGS. The 3rd Heavy Field Artillery Brigade left its garrison at Chiba in Japan on 7 July 1939, and this was before it was shipped to Pusan, Korea. Arriving in the battle zone on 18 July, the brigade which included two fully motorised regiments was considered as somewhat of an elite force among the Artillery Corps. The 1st Heavy Field Artillery Regiment was made up a force of 1,600, it had 100 tractors, 104 trucks, 21 cars, six motorcycles, 10 observation vehicles and three repair trucks, all dedicated to maintaining and operating the 16 howitzers dispersed in its two battalions. These weapons were the brand-new Type 96 15cm howitzers based on a Schneider design with a maximum range of 11,890 metres. The 7th Heavy Field Artillery Regiment was organised similarly, but it was equipped with 16 Type 92 105mm guns. This piece of ordnance was also based on a Schneider design, and, in theory, it could fire a shell at some 18,200 metres. However, firing at maximum range, that is at full charge, generated a very high recoil load, and could break he weapon trails. This flaw in the Type 92 carriage had not been detected before its deployment at Nomonhan because the lack of long-range firing ranges in Japan had seldom allowed the crew to fire at maximum range. Indeed, Japanese gunners rarely trained to fire at targets more than 8,000 metres away. In essence, this meant that once engaged in combat, the 7th Heavy Field Artillery Regiment crew could fire at 13,000 metres at most because they had to avoid using full propellant charges to preserve their ordnance. To add good measure, the Kwantung Army itself deployed to Nomonhan an ad-hoc unit, the Muleng, or Provisional, Heavy Artillery Battalion, which consisted of two batteries of two Type 89 150mm guns. It had been reinforced with another two-gun battery drawn from Port Arthur. The Japanese also massed roughly 245 tons of ammunition, or around 70 percent of the related Kwantung Army artillery stocks.

On the arrival of these reinforcements, the Japanese placed their artillery under Major General Uchiyama Eitaro, the Kwantung

IJA Type 89 150mm guns captured at the end of the Incident. (Albert Grandolini Collection)

A Soviet tank crew inspecting an abandoned Type 95 tank. It demonstrates first-hand how inferior this design was compared to the BT-5 and 7 tanks. (Albert Grandolini Collection)

Army's senior artillery officer. The artillery was divided between two artillery groups, one part was assigned to the 3rd Heavy Field Artillery Brigade, a unit commanded by Major General Hata Yuzaburo and comprising the 1st and 7th Heavy Field Artillery Regiments, reinforced with the Provisional Heavy Battalion. The second, led by Colonel Ise Takahide, comprised units already in place: the 13th Field Artillery Regiment and the 1st Independent Field Artillery Regiment. Both could count on the support of the 1st Artillery Intelligence Regiment, a dedicated outfit which included photographic and meteorological groups and Survey, Light, Sound locating and Train companies. An observation balloon company was also dispatched to the area for spotting purposes. Altogether, the Japanese had amassed a total of 82 guns and howitzers from 75 to 150mm calibres (not including infantry guns) as well as 14,000 shells, including 4,800 105mm rounds for Type 92s, 900 for the Type 89 canons and 4,000 for the Type 96 howitzers.

The influx of firepower was intended to neutralise the so far omnipotent Soviet artillery and thus allow the 23rd Division infantry to launch a successful all-out assault against the Soviet bridgehead to crush it in a matter of hours. There were, however, several crucial flaws in this heavy artillery deployment, most of these caused by the Army's lack of experience in fighting against well-equipped first-tier opponents. Gunners not only lacked training when it came to long-range firing, but in counterbattery skills too. The lack of

cooperation with the Army Air Corps – the latter seldom having trained artillery spotters – was, for instance, to prove a major hindrance. Perhaps more importantly, the Japanese massively underestimated the gargantuan amounts of shells needed to sustain protracted and massive artillery barrages and overestimated the effects of artillery fire. They, therefore, concluded that they could prevail in a matter of two or three days at most in their forthcoming duel with Soviet gunners.

Ironically, they were confidently preparing to take on an enemy that held several major assets on their side. For example, by 1 July, three battalions from the 175th and 185th Artillery regiments were covering the bridgehead disposing of 12 M1934 152mm howitzers, eight M1930 122mm howitzers and fourteen 76mm M1927 and M1930 regimental guns. Of course, Soviet artillery had been reinforced since early July, the Japanese themselves estimating that the enemy had 76 artillery pieces from 100mm to 150mm covering the bridgehead by 22 July. Furthermore, the Soviets' much superior logistical capabilities allowed them to stockpile amounts of ammunition unthinkable for the Japanese. The Soviets had a qualitative advantage too, as their 122mm and 152mm artillery outranged the heaviest Japanese guns by a wide margin. Worst was perhaps the fact that the RKKA artillery was located on higher ground that its IJA counterpart, and that most of its batteries were on reverse slope and thus hidden from direct sight. The Japanese tested an entire array of solutions to locate enemy gun positions, and even managed to get a precise idea of the latter by 22 July, but their efforts could not be sustained once the Soviets began to change their positions. Detection using muzzle flashes or sound was rather imprecise by nature, and the observation towers erected by the Japanese artillerymen were invariably first choice targets and much too low to provide a full view of the heights on the western shore of the Halha River. The contested airspace hardly allowed for low-speed loitering reconnaissance aircraft, and the single balloon deployed during the battle (number 101, made of blue silk) was vulnerable to fire once it had reached an altitude of 1,000 metres. In effect, it was shot down in short order by Soviet fighter aircraft despite it being protected by AA batteries. With this, Soviet artillerymen demonstrated that they had an immense advantage in terms of what would nowadays be termed situational awareness.

For the forthcoming offensive, the 23rd Division had organised itself into two main wings and a separate detachment with both the right and the left wings operating on the northern side of the Holsten River. From north to south, an isolated detachment was guarding the Fui Heights together with a Manchukuoan cavalry force but had no offensive role. The Right Wing composed of the 26th Infantry Regiment, the Left Wing group was commanded by Major General Kobayashi Koichi and was by far the most powerful; it included the 64th and 72nd Infantry Regiments and the 24th Engineer Regiment. The Nagano Detachment was located south of the Holsten River

Table 8: Japanese Artillery Corps Order of Battle, 23 July 1939

Unit	Subunits	Notes
Artillery Corps		CO Major General Uchiyama Eitaro
	1st Artillery Intelligence Regiment	
	Observation Balloon Company	Two balloons
1st Artillery Group		CO Major General Hata Yuzaburo
	1st Heavy Field Artillery Regiment	CO Colonel Mishima Guchiro. Two battalions with 16 Type 96 150mm Howitzers
	7th Heavy Field Artillery Regiment	CO Colonel Takatsukasa Nobuhiro. Two battalions with 16 Type 92 105mm guns. The 2nd Battalion was detached to support the 71st Infantry Regiment
	Muleng Heavy Artillery Battalion	Three batteries with six Type 89 150mm guns
2nd Artillery Group		CO Colonel Ise Takahide
	13th Field Artillery Regiment	Three battalions with 36 Type 38 75mm guns and Type 38 120mm howitzers. The 1st Battalion was detached to support the 71st Infantry Regiment
	1st Independent Field Artillery Regiment	CO Colonel Miyao Kan. Two batteries with eight Type 90 75mm field guns.

infantrymen who had grown used to being on the receiving end of such weapons. For the Japanese, the plan was to use a bombardment to neutralise the Soviet artillery by 1000 hours, the time at which the infantry was to charge enemy lines.

However, Major General Uchiyama Eitaro decided to prolong the artillery barrage for another hour. This decision failing to reach several Japanese infantry battalions that attacked according to the initial plan. It threw the infantry assault into disarray as the first Japanese units to charge soon found themselves targeted by raking fire emanating from positions due to be attacked by other units an hour later. The Soviets, then, were able to concentrate their fire on the first wave of Japanese troops for a full hour. Still, by mid-afternoon, the 26th Infantry Regiment had managed to seize two hills and the 64th Infantry Regiment had managed to reach the periphery of Point 733. The exception rather than the rule, Soviets guns remained silent for a period of the afternoon, and this gave the Japanese artillerymen the impression that they had won. As it turned out, the silence of the guns was due simply to the batteries targeted by the 1st Artillery Group settling into fresh positions where they would not be detected. Once they had done so, they unleashed a murderous barrage against the Japanese, firing three rounds for every one fired by the Japanese. By evening, the four Japanese regiments were pinned down, even though the 72nd Infantry Regiment managed to reach positions a mere 3 kilometres away from the confluence between the Holsten and the Halha Rivers – the very core of the Soviet bridgehead. On the southern side of the Holsten, the 71st Infantry Regiment had only managed to advance a few kilometres before becoming stalled by fierce Soviet counterattacks. The assault still succeeded into forcing the 1st Army Group to dispatch reinforcements to the eastern shore – in the guise of the 2nd Battalion, 601st Rifle Regiment.

and was mainly made up of the 71st Infantry Regiment reinforced with two artillery battalions drawn from the 7th Heavy Field Artillery and 13th Field Artillery Regiments. Its main task was to block any Soviet armoured advance attempting to outflank the entire Japanese line, and it had been sent to beef-up the Hsingan Cavalry Division which had shown time and again its inability to face the enemy armour head-on. The 23rd Division kept a small reserve consisting of the 2nd Battalion, 28th Infantry Regiment and the 23rd Engineer Regiment. The Japanese were confident that a combined attack from their four infantry regiments would allow them to reach the Halha River in two hours. Things were, in reality, no more promising for the infantry than for the artillery as, once more, the same regiments were to be used to assault the Soviet lines. Having received a total of 1,160 reinforcements on 14 July – this was to partially compensate for the losses suffered from 2-12 July – they were weakened by an amoebic dysentery epidemic caused by the lack of potable water. Even worse, the reinforcements sent by the Soviets during the previous assaults had ample time to settle and had dug a series of strong defensive positions. The Soviet lines were now almost continuous, strongly held, and the withdrawal of the 1st Tank Group had given the Soviets complete supremacy in terms or armour: at this point in the battle, they had at least 400 armoured vehicles available.[21]

A Failed Last Hurrah

Unsurprisingly, the would-be decisive offensive ended in yet another dismissal failure in short order. After having been postponed for a few days because of heavy rains, the offensive began at last at 0630 hours on 23 July. It started with the 2nd Artillery Group shelling the Soviet lines to draw up Soviet counterbattery fire to allow Japanese spotters to confirm the enemy batteries positions. Once these had been noted, the 1st Artillery Group "Heavies" opened fire against the Soviet artillery and bridges triggering the enthusiasm of the

The whole affair was to be repeated on 24 July except that, this time, Japanese artillerymen had to lower their rate of fire because of their dwindling stocks of ammunition. It is not surprising, then, that the infantry failed to make any new significant advance. By 24 July, Soviet artillery supremacy was such that several infantry commanders whose units were entrenched near artillery batteries requested the latter to cease fire lest they attract counterbattery fire which, more often than not, fell on their own soldiers. By evening, Lieutenant General Komatsubara concluded that pursuing the offensive was pointless and would only increase the number of casualties for no gain. The events of the next day were to prove him right: not only were the Japanese advanced units targeted by sustained and armoured-supported counterattacks, but the two artillery groups had consumed 80 percent of their stocks of shells and did not have any hope of being resupplied in the short run.

The 71st Infantry Regiment was nonetheless ordered to continue its advance only to be decimated by large-sized counterattacks heavily supported by artillery. The 23rd Division units finally withdrew toward their initial positions at the end of the day, and this was after having suffered heavy casualties for not much gain. Losing nine of their precious guns to enemy counterbattery fire, the Japanese believed they had destroyed 24 pieces of heavy enemy artillery. This estimate proved to be incorrect, and the Soviets lost only 13 pieces: eight 122mm and four 152mm guns and howitzers. They did, however, sustain 3,000 casualties.[22]

The Essentials

The offensive that took place from 23 to 25 July was the last Japanese attempt to wipe out the Soviet foothold on the eastern bank. A week before, Lieutenant General Isogai Rensuke, the Chief of Staff of the Kwantung Army, was summoned to Tokyo where on 20 July he met the Deputy Chief of the Army General Staff and the Vice-Minister of War. He was introduced to a new set of instructions that were formulated as recommendations which explained how it was thought the Nomonhan Incident should be addressed. They were as follows:

ESSENTIALS FOR THE SETTLEMENT OF THE NOMONHAN INCIDENT

The Nomonhan Incident is to be settled in accordance with these Essentials, based upon IGHQ Army Order No. 320 and IGHQ Army Directive No. 491. When situations arise which are difficult to handle according to the Essentials, measures shall be determined on a basis of expediency.

Operational Policy
Efforts will be made to settle the Incident by the coming winter at the latest in accordance with the policy of localising the affair.

Operational Essentials
1. Ground Operations: efforts will be made to wipe out the enemy on the right bank sector of the Halha River.

If the Army achieves the desired battle results; or if diplomatic negotiations reach agreement while the above-mentioned operations are in process; or if the dispute is protracted until winter, efforts will be made to evacuate troops from the disputed area at the earliest opportunity.
Even if Soviet troops enter the disputed zone subsequent to our withdrawal, no punitive ground operations will be carried out again until the situation warrants.

2. Air Operations: The Army will adopt a policy of shooting down enemy aircraft which cross the border and will endeavour to preserve its combat strength. Even if hostile planes bomb Manchukuoan territory, no reprisal attacks will be staged against enemy bases.

3. Efforts will be made to seize the opportunity to initiate diplomatic negotiations as soon as possible, depending upon the progress of operations; and to steer the parleys toward the demarcation of boundary lines and the establishment of demilitarised zones. Negotiations which might lead to the rupture of diplomatic relations will not be conducted.

4. Efforts will be made to bring about an early solution of issues concerning Great Britain; and relations between Japan, Germany and Italy.

5. Strict precautions will be taken to avoid the recurrence of border disputes prior to the settlement of the present Incident.[23]

It was thus made crystal clear that diplomacy would prevail even at the cost of giving up the contested area to the Soviets. Indeed, Lieutenant General Isogai had been summoned precisely to make certain that the *Essentials* were understood as orders by the Kwantung Army. The reception of the *Essentials* did not, however, prevent the Kwantung Army from unleashing an offensive on 23 July, but its failure obviously sealed the fate of any new large-scale attempt to expel the Soviets from the contested area. Furthermore, the incident was to be concluded one way or another as winter was approaching. Sometimes it came early as testified by snow falls that were frequent in September. In view of the freezing conditions, winter was hardly optimal for offensive operations. Another point was that the Japanese believed they were at a disadvantage as they thought both Soviet and Mongolian forces were more able to operate in such conditions. The Japanese therefore give up any pretensions of being able to launch an offensive and began to dig their own defensive positions. By 25 July, even Lieutenant General Komatsubara was having second thoughts about attempting a renewed attack. This, at least, is what can be deduced from the remorseful tone seen in extracts from his own personal diary:

How can I ever destroy the enemy and accomplish my mission in these circumstances? Frontline positions must be built up and battle waged for a protracted period, and I have no adequate words to console the spirits of the many fallen heroes who have sacrificed themselves in hard-fought night attacks advancing to the riverbank for the purpose of destroying what was left of the enemy. I regret that I did not continue the (original) offensive without expecting any assistance from the artillery. I erred.[24]

A new command, the 6th Army, was set up on 4 August, and it was placed under Lieutenant General Ogisu Ryuhei, an officer whose area of responsibility included the Nomonhan area. While the need of such a command had been identified some time before, the rush to put it in place was the consequence of the AGS wanting to take a degree of control over the situation by adding a command layer between the 23rd Division and the Kwantung Army Staff. In practice, the result was that it merely complexified the chain of command and Lieutenant General Ogisu gained only limited influence over the events because the newly raised army command had a very limited number of staff. The Japanese had now given the initiative to the Soviets and were waiting for a diplomatic settlement.[25]

4

OF FALCONS AND EAGLES

The Imperial Japanese Army first acquainted itself with heavier-than-air aircraft during the Russo-Japanese War when it used balloons during the siege of Port Arthur. This was followed by the Army and the Navy creating the Rinji Gunyo Kikyu Kenkyukai (Provisory Military Balloon Research Association) on 30 July 1909, however, having designed several balloons this association was dissolved in 1919. The Army acquired its first aeroplanes in April 1910 (a Maurice Farman HF.2 and a Hans Grade monoplane), Japan's first official domestic flight took place on 19 December of the same year, when Captain Tokugawa Yoshitoshi took off in the Farman at Yoyogi Parade grounds in Tokyo. The following year, the Army set up a military air unit comprising the Farman, the Hans Grade, a Blériot XI-2b and a Wright biplane imported at the beginning of the year. The unit grew steadily over the following years and by the time war broke out in 1914 it had 16 aircraft. Copies of the Farman MF.7, renamed Mo-13, were first delivered in 1914, and the unit's first and only action took place when a provisional detachment of one balloon, four Farmans and one Nieuport NG was sent to support the Japanese troops besieging German-held Tsingtao in August 1914. Japanese airmen remained largely unaware of the fast-paced

French-made SPAD XIII fighters just after their induction into the IJAAC. (Open source)

The Faure military mission shortly after its arrival in Japan. French instructors were instrumental in the Japanese airmen acquiring the skills and experience of combat from the First World War. (Open source)

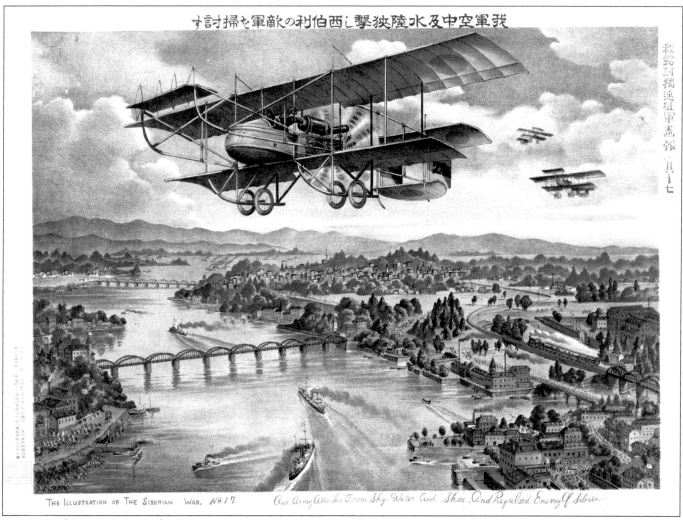

我空軍中及水陸狹擊し西伯利の敵軍を掃討す

THE ILLUSTRATION OF THE SIBERIAN WAR. №17   Our Army Attacks From Sky, Water And Shore, And Repulsed Enemy Of Siberia.

救露討獨遠征軍畫報(其十七

A depiction of Army Farman aircraft in Siberia. (Open source)

developments in aerial warfare that were taking place in Europe. Meanwhile, the Army continued to produce its own aircraft, the Mo-4 and Mo-6, which were variants of the obsolete Farman MF.11.

Coming of Age

It was only in November 1917 that the Japanese Army obtained more modern equipment with the acquisition of two Nieuport 24 C1s and one Spad VII fighter from France in November 1917, followed by other small deliveries the following year. Up to that point Japanese air forces had been backed up by the local fabrication of balloons. In 1915, this led to the creation of the first Hiko Daitai (air battalion) consisting of an air unit and a balloon unit. A second battalion was created in November 1917 followed by a third in December 1918. Nevertheless, the Army's air power remained limited with only 14 Mo-4s and Mo-6s plus nine Sopwith 1½ Strutters being deployed to support the Japanese Expeditionary Corps deployed to Siberia in summer 1918. To increase air power, the Japanese accepted a French offer to send flight instructors. The Frenchmen arriving in January 1919, the next step consisted of Japan ordering more than 220 French-made Spad XIIIs, Bréguet XIV B2s, Salmson 2-A.2s and Caudron R11 aircraft. The influx of equipment and knowhow allowed the Japanese to make up at least some ground on developments that had passed them by during the war. The French mission, comprising some 60 instructors, taught their pupils the arcane arts of flying reconnaissance missions and air combat. Also teaching telegraphy skills or those linked to bombing missions and aircraft maintenance,

the French were instrumental in setting up specialised fighter and reconnaissance units during their nine-month presence in Japan.[1]

The support provided by France enabled the Army's air capabilities to double in size. The 5th Hiko Daitai was set up December 1921 followed by the 4th and the 6th in December 1922. These battalions were made up of two or three chutai (companies) with between 9 and 12 aircraft each. Of the 11 chutai in existence in 1925, five were equipped with fighters and six with reconnaissance aircraft. In 1924, the so-called 'Ugaki' reform led to the disbandment of four divisions and the resulting savings were reallocated for the modernisation of the Army. This allowed for an ambitious development plan including the activation of 10 new chutai, four of them bomber units. The air component gained corps status in 1925, thus becoming the Rikugun Koku Butai (Army Air Corps; IJAAC). In May of the same year, the Air Corps was reorganised with the creation of Hiko Rentai (Air Regiments) which each comprised two battalions. By July 1929, eight Hiko Rentai with 11 fighter, 11 reconnaissance, two light bombers and two heavy bomber chutai were in existence. The expansion continued thereafter, and by the end of 1934 the Corps included 15 fighter, 12 reconnaissance, six light bomber and six heavy bomber chutai. Two years later, the numbers had increased to 21, 12, nine and eight respectively. Organisationally speaking, the activities of the Corps were overseen by four new larger commands: the 1st, 2nd and 3rd Hiko Dan (Air Group, or Air Brigade) controlled the forces stationed in the Home Islands, Korea and Formosa whereas the Hiko Shidan (Air Division) commanded air units attached to the Kwantung Army. However, this doubling in size over roughly

Derived from a Junkers design, the gigantic Ki-20 was the result of a brief attempt by the IJAAC to test strategic bombing in the early 1930s. However, the undertaking ended in utter failure. (Open source)

A Mitsubishi Ki-2 light bomber. These were heavily engaged in China during the first years of conflict. (Open source)

A Nakajima Ki-4. This reconnaissance and light bomber aircraft proved widely popular in the IJAAC, particularly because of its reliability. (Open source)

Combining the reliability and range of a truck with the firepower of a tank, the BA-series of armoured cars was an important part of the Soviet motor-mechanised brigades. Usually painted in olive green, the BA-10s of Soviet units deployed in the Khalkhin Gol area wore either no markings, or a bare minimum. They were replaced in the scouting role by light tanks during the Second World War. (Artwork by David Bocquelet)

Having the same firepower and similar armour to the T-26 tank, but with a large V-12 engine and Christie suspension, the BT-7 was the most powerful tank deployed during the Nomonhan conflict. As usual, all were painted in olive green, and they wore either no, or only a bare minimum of markings. While performing well against the Japanese, the BT-7 series performed poorly against the Germans in 1941 and was replaced by the T-34 during the Second World War. Ironically, dozens remained in the RKKA inventories long enough to take part in the August Storm operation in 1945. (Artwork by David Bocquelet)

The Type 89 I-Go medium tank was a curious mix of old and new concepts. It had the archaic lines of a first-generation tank, but a relatively advanced diesel engine. The low-velocity 57mm gun had a high-explosive load which could not penetrate modern armour but would pop the rivets on enemy tanks, wounding the crew members inside. Their worst default, however, was – like all the other types of Japanese tanks deployed during the Nomonhan Incident – their single-man turret. The tank commander was supposed to lead his vehicle while loading and firing the main gun or the turret machine gun. Like their Soviet-operated opponents, Japanese tanks in the Nomonhan conflict were usually painted in dark green, and wore either no, or only a minimum of insignia. (Artwork by David Bocquelet)

A young sergeant and Ki-27 pilot of the 11th Sentai based in the Harbin area of China, May 1939. In his hand is a 'Type 95 shin-gunto', a less sophisticated version of the military sword distributed to NCOs from 1935. There is at least one known case where a Japanese pilot used such a weapon to dispatch his shot down Soviet counterpart. Over his regular uniform of the Imperial Japanese Army, he is shown wearing one of the earliest versions of the winter flight suit. It is easily recognisable from the flaps covering the pockets on the legs (deleted on subsequent versions). The fur-lined flight cap and goggles were both introduced in 1937 while the harness is for the Type 95 seat-parachute. The gloves appear to be the leather-lined model, and the flight boots had moulded rubber soles for better grip on the cockpit pedals. Many Japanese pilots preferred to carry their own personal weapon and, usually an 8mm Nambu Type 14 pistol was simply tucked into the belt or attached to the life jacket. (Artwork by Anderson Subtil)

A Senior Private of the 72nd Infantry Regiment as seen at the Kawatama Bridge in July 1939. As of this time, the IJA had already introduced the Type 98 uniform that became widespread during the subsequent war in the Pacific. However, most of the troops involved in the Nomonhan War still wore old Showa 5 (or Type 90) uniforms – probably due to logistical snags – as shown here. This was made of light khaki cotton fabric, with the red infantry insignia sewn to the tunic's collars. The steel helmet is the Model 1932, and in this case, it is placed atop the characteristic field cap made from fabric. Leg wrappers/puttees are of the old type while short boots were of the more recent Type 98. The soldier is shown with a good quantity of individual equipment including a backpack, metal kettle, the trench shovel, a blanket, and a tarpaulin (used as a raincoat and as a tent section). The haversack is of the 1932 pattern. Visible is a bag for a gas mask, and two cartridge pouches, the sheath for the Type 30 long bayonet and a bag for the cleaning utensils for his 6.5mm Arysaka Type 38 rifle. (Artwork by Anderson Subtil)

This Lieutenant Colonel of the 13th Field Artillery Regiment (deployed during the Japanese offensive of July 1939) is shown wearing the winter version of the Showa 5 uniform made of green wool fabric. This included tunic and trousers of a similar design to those of the soldier shown above, but slightly more elegant. Notable is the large yellow insignia of the Artillery Corps sewn to the collar and the white cloth gloves, typical of Japanese officers. The leather straps across the chest were used to attach a canteen, binoculars box and the Type 26 revolver holster. The officer is shown holding his shin-gunto, and several times during the Nomonhan conflict Japanese officers used these when attacking Soviet tanks by climbing atop of them, opening hatches and killing their crews. Finally, he is shown wearing officer's boots, although ankle boots and knee-length gaiters were quite popular. (Artwork by Anderson Subtil)

Following the local warrior traditions, the small Mongolian Army consisted of – essentially – cavalry troops like this one. Most of their clothing consisted of whatever pieces they could get from the Red Army (green for the summer and brown for the winter), with the only obvious change being the collar badges. Their armament was also Soviet: a 7.62mm calibre M1891/30 Mosin Nagant bolt-action rifle – the standard weapon of the Soviet infantry in late 1930s. The primary mount was the small, sturdy and fast Mongolian horse or pony – essentially still unchanged since the tempestuous times of Genghis Khan in the thirteenth century: they offered mobility on the vast plains of eastern Mongolia but proved hopelessly vulnerable to artillery and automatic weapons. (Artwork by Anderson Subtil)

Despite being referred to in much of the existing literature as a general, at the time of the Nomonhan conflict Georgy Zhukov held the title of Corps Commander. The tile of general officer was reintroduced to the Red Army only on the eve of the Nazi invasion in 1941 when Zhukov was promoted to Army General. This illustration reproduces his uniform during one of the troop inspections in mid-1939 and includes the summer model of the traditional Russian *gymnastiorka* in green. His rank insignia in yellow, and triangles in red brass (also called 'diamonds') on the blue background with yellow border on the collars identify him as a cavalry officer. He still wore the Sam Browne-style belt, very widespread in the 1930s, and characterised as a wide, usually leather belt, supported by a narrow diagonal strap over the right shoulder. The semi-breeches – known to the Red Army as *sharovari* – are shown in black although their most usual colour was dark blue. (Artwork by Anderson Subtil)

This Captain from the 11th Tank Brigade was the commander in one of the BT-7 units deployed to Mongolia in July and August 1939. He is shown wearing the typical Red Army tank overall of the 1930s influenced by Germany and France. The characteristic padded crash helmet was based on a model used by German pilots in the First World War, and it provided no protection from small arms fire or shell fragments, but only from the shrarp edges of the interior of the tank (travelling at speed in a cramped metal environment over rough terrain made this an almost essential item of equipment and photographs showing tank crews without them are very rare). Over the *gymnastiorka* he donned a leather overcoat – probably of French origin and acquired by the Russians during the last years of the Tsarist period. On each collar are the black and red service colours of the armoured corps complemented by vertical bars in red – indicating the rank of Captain – and a metallic badge representing a tank. The belt and holster for the Nagant M1905 revolver are of 1935 standard while the shoulder bag carried the BN1932 gas mask. Notable are the thick leather gloves (probably of the same origin as the overcoat), and ubiquitous knee boots. All of this heavy clothing was usually replaced by simple overalls of striking blue fabric in milder climates. (Artwork by Anderson Subtil)

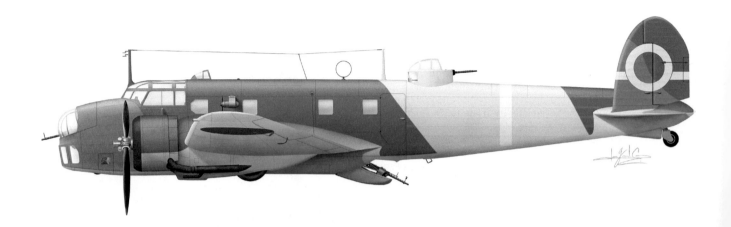

A Fiat BR.20 of the 12th Hiko Sentai, 7th Hiko Dan at Nomonhan. Japan bought 72 of these bombers from Italy to make up for the delayed induction of the Mitsubishi Ki-21. None were shot down during the war with the USSR, but one was damaged beyond economic repair. (Artwork by Luca Canossa)

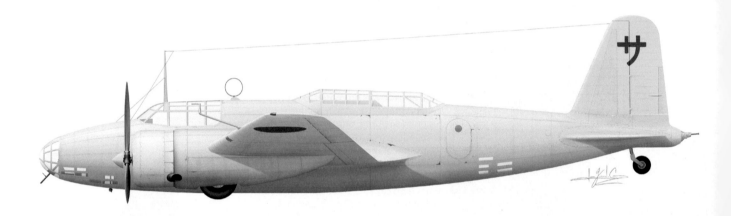

A Mitsubishi Ki-21 of the 61st Hiko Sentai, 9th Hiko Dan, at Nomonhan. These domestically produced bombers suited Japanese military philosophies of the time and came to be preferred over the Fiat. They were fast and could evade interception. The Japanese claimed no losses, but there are Soviet photos of a shot down Ki-21. (Artwork by Luca Canossa)

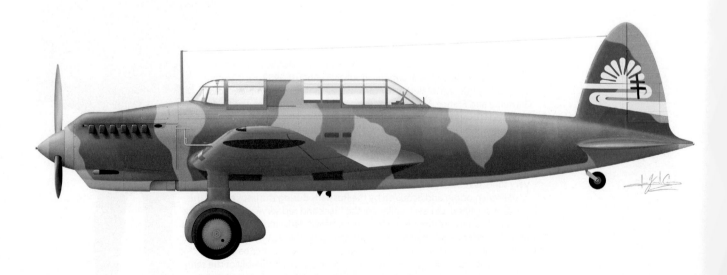

A Kawasaki Ki-32 light bomber of the 16th Hiko Sentai, 9th Hiko Dan. Due to their light handling, the Ki-32 was preferred by pilots over the similar Mitsubishi Ki-30. However, the inline engine frequently overheated and – due to its liquid cooling – was vulnerable to combat damage. (Artwork by Luca Canossa)

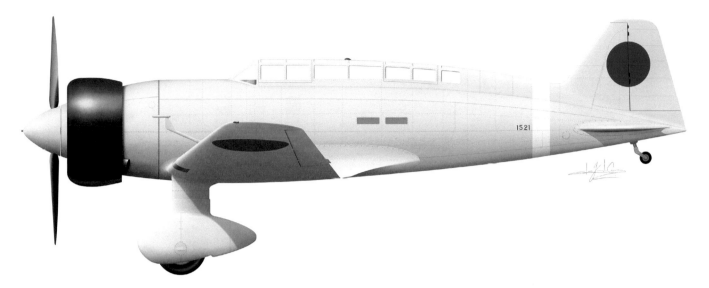

A Mitsubishi Ki-15 of the 15th Hiko Sentai, 12th Hiko Dan. This fast reconnaissance aircraft of the late 1930s was designed to penetrate the enemy airspace, and to take photos of their targets and escape before they could be intercepted. Nevertheless, at least six Ki-15s were shot down during the Nomonhan War, and seven others written off due to combat damage. (Artwork by Luca Canossa)

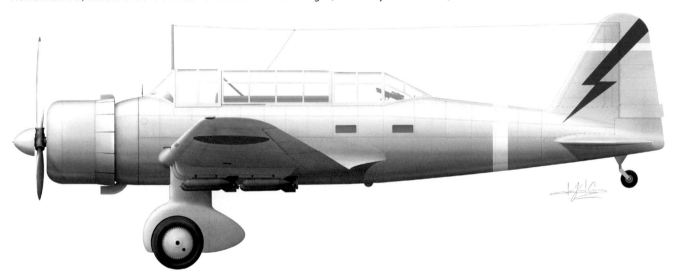

A Mitsubishi Ki-30 of the 16th Sentai, 9th Hiko Dan. This was a combat effective light bomber, capable of operating from rough terrain. After Nomonhan, it was used in the early stages of the Second World War, but then relegated to training duties after the Philippines campaign. Eleven were shot down and seven written off over Nomonhan. (Artwork by Luca Canossa)

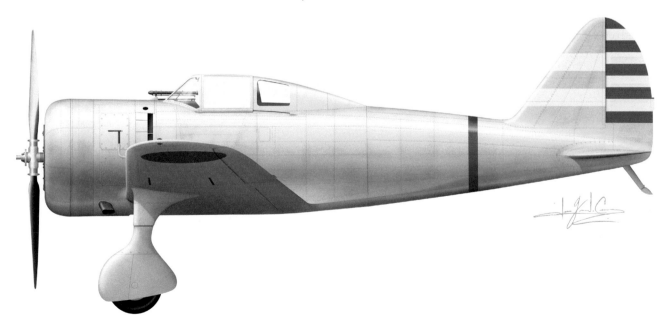

A Nakajima Ki-27 of the 24th Sentai. This lightweight fighter was supreme for the first half of the conflict but suffered increasing losses as experienced Soviet pilots with more advanced versions of the I-16 arrived at the front. By the end of the conflict 62 had been shot down with another 34 written off – most often with tragic consequences for their pilots. (Artwork by Luca Canossa)

The Kawasaki Ki-10 was the standard Japanese Army Air Force fighter prior to the introduction of the Ki-27. By mid-1939, most of these were being used as advanced trainers but others still equipped several first-line units. One was shot down, but one also scored a (rather surprising) aerial victory. (Artwork by Luca Canossa)

The Polikarpov R-5 was the standard light reconnaissance aircraft of the Soviet and Mongolian air forces. It was also used as a light bomber. They saw widespread combat deployment during the Nomonhan conflict, and a number were lost to Japanese fighters and to ground fire. (Artwork by Luca Canossa)

The Tupolev SB-2 was the 'star' of the Soviet air force during the Nomonhan conflict. This twin-engined light bomber not only bore the brunt of the bombing campaign against the Japanese troops, but also proved fast and capable of surviving combat damage. Nevertheless, 44 were shot down by Japanese fighters and anti-aircraft guns. (Artwork by Luca Canossa)

The Polikarpov I-15bis proved no match for most of the Japanese fighters over Nomonhan: it was too slow and lacked manoeuvrability in comparison to the Ki-27. Unsurprisingly, up to 60 were shot down during the war with Japan. Most of the aircraft that saw service during this war wore camouflage colours shown here, and they consisted of dark olive green on top surfaces and sides, and light admiralty grey on undersurfaces. National markings were usually applied in six positions. Such 'means of easier identification' – as officially known in the USSR – like fin-tips and spinners painted in red became quite widespread during the Nomonhan conflict. (Artwork by Luca Canossa)

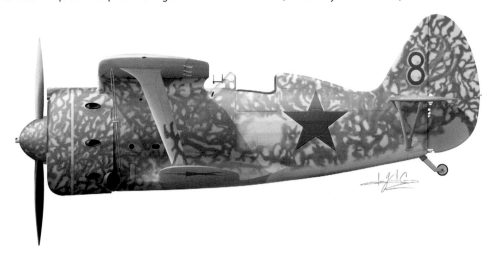

The Polikarpov I-153 was the result of an attempt by Nikolai Polikarpov to convert the obsolete biplane into an aircraft viable in modern air combat. While it included a retractable undercarriage and other improvements to reduce drag, it was vulnerable to fast, manoeuvrable monoplanes like the Ki-27. Most of the I-153s deployed during the Nomonhan War only received hastily applied camouflage patterns consisting of dark green or olive green applied with help of spray gun around their existing markings. A total of 16 I-153s were shot down during the short conflict. (Artwork by Luca Canossa)

The Polikarpov I-16 Type 10 was the most advanced Soviet fighter-interceptor of the Nomonhan conflict. It was armed with four improved ShKAS machine guns, rather than the Type 5's two, and powered by an uprated engine. When flown by experienced pilots it proved capable of holding its own against the Ki-27. The majority of I-16s deployed during the Nomonhan conflict were painted in dark olive green with light admiralty grey on the undersurfaces, and they had the national insignia applied in six positions. In addition to the 'bort' number ('white 33'), this aircraft received an identification stripe in white around the rear fuselage. (Artwork by Luca Canossa)

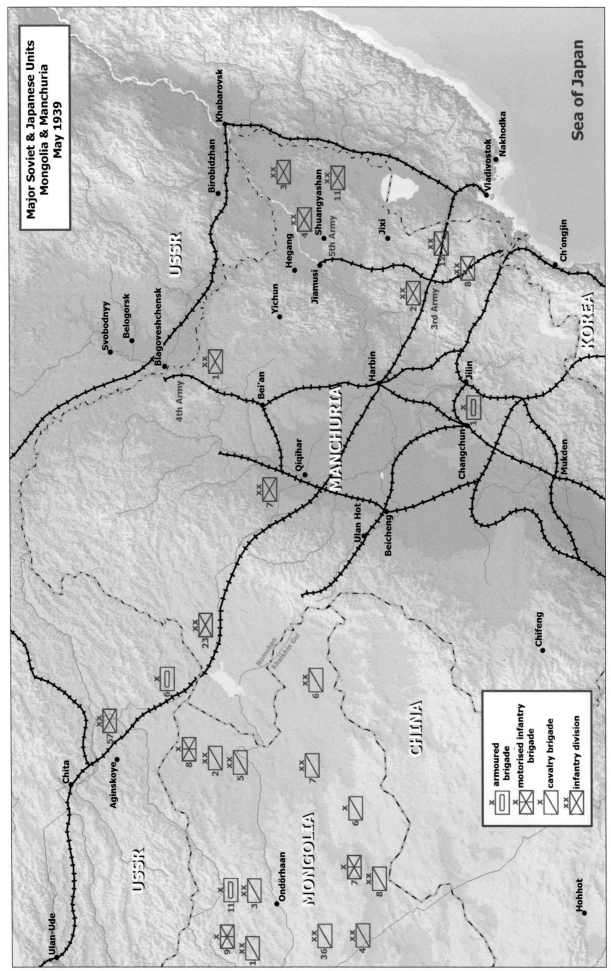

Major Soviet & Japanese Units
Mongolia & Manchuria
May 1939

A map of eastern Mongolia, north-eastern China (including what used to be the quisling-state Manchukuo, in Manchuria), and south-eastern Soviet Union with mutual borders, major railroads, and original positions of major ground units as at the start of the Nomonhan conflict. (Map by Tom Cooper)

Table 9: Imperial Japanese Air Corps Order of Battle, 1936[3]		
Units	**Location**	**Notes**
1st Hiko Dan		Covering Japanese Home Islands
1st Hiko Rentai	Kagamigahara	Four fighter chutai
2nd Hiko Rentai	Kagamigahara	Two reconnaissance chutai
3rd Hiko Rentai	Yokaichi	Three reconnaissance chutai
7th Hiko Rentai	Hamamatsu	First bombing unit of the IJAAC, raised in 1925. Two light bomber chutai and two heavy bomber chutai
13th Hiko Rentai	Kakogawa	Three fighter chutai
2nd Hiko Dan		Covering Korea
6th Hiko Rentai	Pyongyang	One fighter chutai, two light bomber chutai
9th Hiko Rentai	Hoeryong	Two fighter chutai, two light bomber chutai
3rd Hiko Dan		Covering Formosa
8th Hiko Rentai	Pingtung	One fighter chutai, one light bomber chutai
14th Hiko Rentai	Chaii	Two heavy bomber chutai
4th Hiko Rentai	Tachiarai	Two fighter chutai, two reconnaissance chutai
5th Hiko Rentai	Tachikawa	Two fighter chutai, two reconnaissance chutai
Kantogun Hiko Shidan		Attached directly to the Kwantung Army (Kantogun) HQ. Covering Manchuria. Around 230 aircraft
10th Hiko Rentai	Tsitsihar	Three light bomber chutai
11th Hiko Rentai	Harbin	Four fighter chutai
12th Hiko Rentai	Gongzhuling	Four heavy bomber chutai
15th Hiko Rentai	Changchun	Three reconnaissance chutai
16th Hiko Rentai	Mutanchiang	Two fighter chutai, two light bomber chutai

five years did not satisfy the Army hierarchy and a new development programme to create a further 89 chutai over the next six years was implemented.[2]

Aerial Exterminating Action

The 1919 French mission heavily influenced the doctrine of the nascent air corps. Artillery Colonel Jacques Paul Faure proved to be a particularly conservative figure putting the emphasis on tactical ground support. The artillery, in his view, being much more efficient in providing fire support, the air corps' priority was to carry out reconnaissance and aerial combat missions. This was because fighter aircraft were deemed necessary for both the escort of allied reconnaissance aircraft and the interception of enemy aircraft, with ground attacks being a low priority. Faure argued that giving the aviation corps status would harm an officer's career due to its limited perspectives, while it was considered much better for the air wing to be staffed by officers from another corps such as the artillery, the cavalry, and the infantry as they brought an intimate knowledge

A Kawasaki Ki-10 with its characteristic air-cooled engine. A potent fighter at the time, it had grown obsolete by 1939. (Open source)

The Mitsubishi Ki-15 "Strategic" reconnaissance aircraft. Its speed made it extremely difficult for fighters such as the I-15 and I-16 to intercept. (Open source)

A row of Chinese Air Force Curtiss Hawk IIIs. Considered a powerful fighter at the beginning of the war, it became obsolete as soon as the Japanese navy and army fielded their respective A5M and Ki-27 fighters. (Open source)

of the needs of their original units and could pass this knowledge on. Naturally, these arguments were milk and honey for the most conservative members of the Japanese officer corps and, therefore, it was only in 1925 that the service attained corps status and that the first bomber chutai were created. This said, by 1929 only four of the latter were operational.

Only at the end of the 1920s did things begin to change. At first, the weakness of the Soviet military presence in the Far East during this decade enticed the Army to study operations against the US-held Philippines as the institution was keen to demonstrate its usefulness and, at the same time, defend its budget allocation against its arch-rival, the Japanese navy. In March 1930, concerns such as these led the Army to order a heavy bomber capable of attacking US bases in the Philippines from Formosa. In turn, this led to the building of the Mitsubishi Ki-20 heavy bomber, an aircraft based on the Junkers K-51 and introduced in 1933. The undertaking eventually petered out and only six machines were ever produced.

Much more significant developments were the Japanese seizure of Manchuria in 1931 and 1932 and the resulting build-up of Red Army aviation in the Far East. Before long, the VVS inventories in the region not only widely outmatched the corresponding IJAAC forces in terms of battle orders in Korea and Manchuria, but they included several units of TB-3 heavy bombers able to target cities in Japan from their airfields in the Soviet Maritime Province. This led the Japanese airmen to conclude that a much more offensive use of airpower at the onset of a conflict was needed to neutralise the VVS to be able to provide the expected tactical ground support. Consequently, the concept of large-scale counter-air operations targeting enemy airfields at an early stage, or 'aerial exterminating action' in IJAAC parlance, was adopted in 1934. This was further refined once Japanese officers under Major General Ohshima Horoshi were sent to Germany to study the Luftwaffe doctrine. The latter also emphasised aggressive and systematic air raids against enemy air bases at the onset of a conflict to swiftly gain air superiority. 'Aerial exterminating action' therefore became the official objective of the

A CAF pilot from the 5th Pursuit Group proudly poses in front of his I-15bis fighter. (Open source)

Air Corps once it was included in the December 1937 edition of the Air Troops Operations manual. This corresponded to an increase in the number of the bomber units, they skyrocketed from four in 1930 to 20 in 1936. In 1934, the IJAAC's ongoing acquisition programme included a five bomber, three fighter and two reconnaissance aircraft force structure ratio.[4]

China Skies

The outbreak of the Chinese Incident forced the IJAAC to commit considerable resources to the Chinese mainland under the aegis of a new provisional air brigade, the Rinji Hiko Dan, led by Lieutenant General

A Nakajima Ki-27 prototype. This fighter turned out to be a mature design right from the outset and remained the workhorse of the IJAAC's fighter arm well into 1941. (Open source)

A Mitsubishi Ki-21 heavy bomber in flight. The entry into service of this aircraft was delayed and forced the IJAAC to purchase Fiat BR.20 bombers from Italy to fill the gap. (Open source)

Baron Tokugawa Yoshitoshi. Soon, no fewer than six fighter, nine reconnaissance, five light bomber and four heavy bomber chutai were engaged in battle. Operating either independently as Dokoritu Hiko Chuta (Independent Flying Chutai) or as parts of eight Hiko Datai, all drawn from existing regiments, these operated a total of 230 aircraft – 100 Kawasaki Ki-10 fighters, 82 Nakajima Ki-4 reconnaissance aircraft, 24 Mitsubishi Ki-2 light bombers and 24 Mitsubishi Ki-1 heavy bombers. The focus of the IJAAC was initially brought to Northern China as the Navy Air Corps was responsible for air operations in Southern China and Central China.

Table 10: Rinji Hiko Dan (Provisional Air Brigade), Summer 1937

Units	Notes
1st Hiko Daitai	Two reconnaissance chutai, Nakajima Ki-4
2nd Hiko Daitai	Two reconnaissance chutai, Nakajima Ki-4
3rd Hiko Daitai	Three fighter chutai, Kawasaki Ki-10
5th Hiko Daitai	Two light bomber chutai, Mitsubishi Ki-2
6th Hiko Daitai	Two heavy bomber chutai, Mitsubishi Ki-1
8th Hiko Daitai	Two fighter chutai, Kawasaki Ki-10
9th Hiko Daitai	Two light bomber chutai, Mitsubishi Ki-2
3rd Dokoritu Hiko Chutai	Heavy bomber, Mitsubishi Ki-1, drawn from the 7th Hiko Rentai
4th Dokoritu Hiko Chutai	Reconnaissance, Nakajima Ki-4, drawn from the 4th Hiko Rentai
6th Dokoritu Hiko Chutai	Reconnaissance, Nakajima Ki-4, drawn from the 4th Hiko Rentai
9th Dokoritu Hiko Chutai	Fighter, Kawasaki Ki-10, drawn from the 6th Hiko Rentai

With initial operations consisting of providing support for ground troops either by targeting frontlines or rear positions and lines of communications, air strikes were also carried out against urban centres usually just before their invasion by ground forces. As for aerial combat, it was only from mid-September 1937 that the airmen came face-to-face with their counterparts from the Chinese Air Force (CAF). On 19 September 1937, the first aerial combat took place when a patrol of four Ki-10 fighters attacked a formation of six CAF Douglas O-38s claiming to have shot down four in a short space of time. From that point, the provisional air group frequently targeted airfields while continuing to fly support missions. Another development that took place from mid-September was the deployment of IJAAC detachments to Central and Southern China where an increasing number of IJA divisions were drawn in the protracted Shanghai battle. This spurred the requirement to complete the command structure. Of three Hiko Dan subsequently established, one was tasked with operating in areas occupied by the Central China Area Army while the other two surveyed the Northern China Area Army.

The IJAAC and pilots of the Japanese navy became increasingly involved in combat with the CAF. Indeed, Chinese units were regularly decimated by a combination of air combats and raids against their airfields, but the vastness of the country allowed them to withdraw exhausted squadrons from the front lines and rebuild them thanks to the influx of aircraft and equipment supplied by the Soviet Union. This supply line became important to Chinese forces, especially at the end of 1938 when the number of Chinese aircraft fell to 281. Out of the more than 600 aircraft available to the CAF in 1937, 166 aircraft had been destroyed in air combat, another 46 on the ground and a further 101 were lost in accidents. The Soviet Union also sent large numbers of pilots and support personnel. They manned several CAF squadrons thus guaranteeing that the battle for the Chinese skies would be arduous and protracted. On a positive note, this meant that hundreds of Japanese fighter pilots gained a wealth of combat experience against aircraft such as the Gladiator, the Hawk III, the Fiat CR.32 or the I-15bis and I-16. The latter of these greatly outmatched the Ki-10, which was replaced by Nakajima Ki-27 fighters that were first used in China in March 1938.

A Ki-27 of the 59th Sentai carrying its drop tank. The Japanese were among the first to implement wide use of these tanks to increase the range of their fighters. (Open source)

A Mitsubishi Ki-30 carrying 50kg bombs under the wing. They added to those in the bomb bay. (Open source)

The Kawasaki Ki-32 was almost the Ki-30's twin. The main difference between the two light bombers was the engine. (Open source)

The Japanese fighters also had plenty of opportunity to attempt the interception of SB bombers sent to attack their airbases.

These developments taken into consideration, it is not surprising that by early 1938 the number of chutai operating in China increased, with 14 operating in Northern China and 10 in Central China. By the end of the year, and after the fall of Wuhan, the Corps took part in a series of long-range air raids against the new Nationalist capital, Chungking, and against Lanzhou, a crucial hub in the delivery of Soviet supplies to the Nationalists. The task of undertaking these raids fell to the 1st Hiko Dan (a unit centred on the 60th, 12th and 98th Sentai) using brand-new Mitsubishi Ki-21 heavy bombers and Fiat BR.20 heavy bombers. Using Hankou as a base, this brigade conducted a series of four night-raids on Chungking in December 1938 and January 1939 before switching its attention to Lanzhou in February. Things did not always go to plan. The city and its airfields were defended by around 100 enemy fighters, and it had become clear that IJAAC airmen were not used to flying at night. They had problems with long-range navigation and found it difficult to coordinate their long-range reconnaissance with heavy bombers. Flying in formation, the bombers tended to split into smaller groups as they approached their targets.

Naturally, the fighters could not escort the bombers throughout the outward and homeward journeys. This left bombers having to fend for themselves during the most dangerous leg of their trip. The result was that first two raids against Lanzhou on 9 and 12 February ended with the loss of five Br.20s. Another attack was made against the airfields surrounding the town on 20 February, and this time it involved 30 aircraft that met with heavy resistance, the Japanese formation having split into three groups and attacking one after the other. As for the Chinese, they quickly scrambled the 15th and 17th Pursuit Squadrons (CAAF) using 15 I-15bis, one I-16 and one Hawk III. Chinese pilots claimed to have shot down nine bombers; it is recorded that the 98th Sentai lost two of its Fiats. Such heavy losses forced the 1st Hiko Dan to eventually call off the operation a few days later.

The Reorganisation of July 1938

The air war over China from 1937 to 1939 remains a relatively unknown, intensive and costly affair, it did though provide the IJAAC with plenty of hard-won lessons which contributed to it becoming an effective fighting machine. The experience led to a major reorganisation of the IJAAC structures in July 1938, and one of the main lessons drawn was that operational mobility and flexibility had to be improved. Ultimately, this led to the abandonment of the chutai-daitai-rentai structure.

As for the daitai and the rentai, they were replaced by a single entity, the *Hiko Sentai* (flying unit, or regiment). In theory, fighter Sentai had three 12 aircraft strong chutai and a sentai hombu (regiment HQ) with three aircraft, bomber sentai had 27 to 36 aircraft with either nine or 12 machines per chutai, and reconnaissance Sentai had from 18 to 27 aircraft, with either six or nine airplanes per chutai. These assets were combined to become Hiko Dan (air brigades) and, in turn, Hiko Shidan (air divisions).

These were operational commands and could be moved at will, while the Sentai and independent companies (Dokuritu Hiko Chutai) could be easily be attached and detached from these according to needs. Furthermore, the existing units were split between mobile and static elements with the Sentai keeping only the pilots, armourers and mechanics; a total of 360 to 600 personnel. To give but one concrete example of this reorganisation, the 8th Hiko Daitai was disbanded on 31 July 1938 leading to the creation of both the 77th Sentai and the 41st Airfield battalion, whilst the 64th Sentai created on 1 August 1938 was an amalgamation of the 2nd Hiko Daitai and the 9th Dokuritu Hiko Chutai. Further reforms saw the Hiko Shidan headquarters gain responsibility for a various number of air sectors which, in turn, were responsible for operating airfields and taking charge of all the logistical aspects. This ensured that Sentai could be moved swiftly from one airfield to another and be operational almost instantly. Thus by 7 August 1938 the Provisional Air Brigade controlled three air brigades, as well as two air sector headquarters which in turn oversaw a total of seven airfield battalions, two airfield companies, seven motorised transport companies, six construction units and two field depots. A much smaller, brigade-sized command dedicated to support the Northern China Area Army controlled the HQs of two air sectors, two airfield battalions, one motor transport company and a construction unit to support its two light bomber Sentai and its single fighter chutai.[5] Once this reorganisation ended in early September 1938, the IJAAC found itself with a total 32 Sentai (11 fighter, nine light bomber, seven heavy bomber and five reconnaissance) as well as three reconnaissance and two fighter *Dokuritsu* (Independent) *Hiko Chutai*.[6]

The Air Corps had, by then, been operating several training schools for several years. The Akeno fighter school was the most famous, but the emphasis was qualitative with highly selective admissions processes and high rates of failure. The pilots received around 300 hours flying time during their training, roughly two-thirds of the trainees were enlisted men with the remainder being officers who had completed their regular army training before switching to the IJAAC. The system produced well-trained pilots from the outset, however these were few and far between. Even by 1941, the IJAAC was only turning out 750 pilots per year making the institution vulnerable given the high rates of attrition brought on by full-fledged air battles between first rate powers, as the Nomonhan Incident illustrated.

Table 11: IJAAC Sentai as of early September 1938[7]	
	Sentai
Fighters	1st, 4th, 5th, 9th, 11th, 13th, 24th, 33rd, 59th, 64th, 77th
Reconnaissance	2nd, 8th, 10th, 15th, 28th
Light Bomber	3rd, 6th, 16th, 27th, 31st, 45th, 65th, 75th, 90th
Heavy Bomber	7th, 12th, 14th, 58th, 60th, 61st, 98th

The Birth of an Industry

Key to the build-up of the Japanese air arm was the successful development of a fully-fledged aeronautics industry. At an early stage, both the Japanese navy and army relied on their own respective arsenals to acquire and master the related technologies. This was to prove temporary in the case of the IJAAC as it stopped the design and production of its own aircraft, preferring, instead, to use aircraft made by different Japanese companies. At the time, several corporations had set up structures to meet the demands of the new and promising military aviation market: Mitsubishi in 1916, Nakajima in 1917, and these were soon followed by Kawasaki, to name but a few. The companies in question did not acquire the necessary knowhow suddenly; they hired the services of foreign experts, sent their own engineers abroad to study aircraft design, and built their own research centres and testing facilities. The new centres produced various models under licence allowing the Japanese to hone their knowledge, and thanks to various forms of cooperation with renowned western firms (such as Dornier or Junkers), the fledging industry gradually became capable of designing and producing its own aircraft, all the while integrating new aircraft technologies that emerged at a rapid pace. A crucial milestone came in 1934 when the Japanese Army adopted the Nakajima Ki-4 reconnaissance aircraft, it became the first aircraft completely designed by the Japanese. In

A rear-view of a Tachikawa Ki-36 liaison aircraft. (Open source)

A Soviet I-16 fighter and its navy ground crew during the Nomonhan Incident. (Open source)

An I-15 showing its characteristic gull-shaped upper-wing. (Open source)

1936, Mitsubishi produced another home-made aircraft, the A5M or Navy Fighter Type 96. On a par with, or superior to, contemporary western fighters, this marked the time when Japan's national air industry came of age. This was made crystal clear worldwide when a Mitsubishi Ki-15 reconnaissance aircraft landed in London on 9 April 1937. Owned by the newspaper *Asahi Shinbun*, the aircraft was equipped with virtually all the latest technology allowing it to make the 15,359 kilometre-flight from Japan in 94 hours and 18 minutes. By 1939, most of the aircraft used by the IJAAC were Japanese-made and equalled, or sometimes out-performed, aircraft produced

by leading manufacturers in the UK, the US or France.[8] Japanese aircraft manufacturers continued to acquire foreign aircraft, but this was usually for testing and evaluation purposes only.

The Army's Birds of Prey
In 1939, the IJAAC fighter arm relied on two distinct aircraft – the Ki-10 and the Ki-27 – the second of these gradually replacing the first. Designed in 1934 by Kawasaki in response to a request by the IJAAC for a new fighter, the Ki-10's inaugural flight took place in March 1935. Officially adopted by the Japanese Army in December

of that year, the new fighter proved to be a very nimble aircraft. Generating 850hp at take-off, its liquid-cooled inline Kawasaki Ha-9-II Ko engine gave it a top speed of 400km/h at an altitude of 3,000 metres. This biplane was also capable of reaching a height of 5,000 metres in five minutes, its armament consisted of two Type 89 7.7mm machine guns, the standard weapons for IJAAC fighters since 1930. The Type 89 was the Japanese version of the Vickers 0.303 Mk III, itself largely derived from the Browning M1922, and it was straightforward to use and reliable. Able to fire between 600 and 900 rounds per minute, rounds travelled at 820 metres per second. In China, the Ki-10 proved more than a match for CAAF fighters such as the Hawk III, the CR.32 or the I-15bis, but it encountered problems when facing the I-16, and even more so intercepting the Chinese and Soviet-flown SB fast bombers. Another of the Ki-10's shortcomings was poor forward stability that hindered the pilot's aim when firing.

In any case, the IJAAC had issued another request in 1935 and, this time, it was to procure a low-wing monoplane with a maximum speed of 450km/h and able to climb to 5,000 metres in less than six minutes. Retaining a manoeuvrability similar to a biplane, it was to be armed with the standard two machine gun set up. Kawasaki, Mitsubishi and Nakajima developed their own prototypes, but it was Nakajima's Ki-27 that was to be favoured thanks to its superior manoeuvrability. Ordered by the IJAAC in December 1937 and

renamed the 'Army Fighter Type 97', the first of these aircraft arrived in China in March 1938 where they first took part in aerial combat on 9 April 1938. This was when three Ki-27s and 12 Ki-10s of the 2nd Hiko Daitai intercepted a total of 18 I-15bis from the CAF's 3rd and 4th Pursuit Groups. One of the three Ki-27s was lost during the action, but two enemy I-15bis were shot down and another severely damaged. In addition to two other prototypes, 743 Ki-27s had been built by the end of 1939 thus allowing for the reequipment of most of the Air Corps' fighter units.

The K-27 was a simple and easy-to-maintain low-wing monoplane with an enclosed cockpit and a fixed undercarriage. It was powered by an air-cooled Nakajima Ha-1 Otsu engine developing 710hp at take-off and could reach a maximum speed of 460km/h at 3,500 metres while climbing at 5,000 metres in 5 minutes and 22 seconds. Nakajima had, indeed, succeeded in designing an extremely manoeuvrable aircraft with a high rate of turn that was easy to control and stable, easing the pilot's task when firing the two Type 89 machine guns fed by 500-round magazines. Proof of this ease came through the American, Claire Lee Chennault, who had the opportunity to test-fly a captured Ki-27 when he served as chief air adviser to Chiang Kai-shek. According to him, the aircraft was "One of the best aerobatic aeroplanes ever built. It climbs like a skyrocket and manoeuvers like a squirrel".[9]

The qualities of the aircraft did, nonetheless, come at a price. Engineers had to keep the aircraft as light as possible (it weighed only 1,110kg empty), and this meant that it was devoid of any armoured protection and lacked robustness. Also, it had a wing loading akin to a biplane (85kg per square metre) to increase its low-speed manoeuvrability. As a result, the fighter was unable to make high-speed dives as these would lead to unsustainable vibrations or even a wing tearing off. All the aircraft were equipped with a radio receiver, but only the leaders had a transmitter. These, moreover, were unreliable, the pilots within a formation continued to rely mostly on hand signals or wing movements for communication. One Japanese pilot who took part in the Nomonhan Incident summarised the attributes of what, by then, had become the workhorse of the Army's fighter arm: "The 97-Sen was easy to fly and very agile. If a pursuer was seen it was easy to climb quickly and return to follow him. On the other hand, it could dive too steeply or too fast without excessive vibration making it difficult to aim properly".[10]

A Polikarpov I-16 during take-off in 1936. By then, it was one of the best fighters of its time as its introduction in Spain was to show. (Open source)

One of the I-153 prototypes, with the retractable train and upper gull-shaped wing easily observable. However, by the time of its introduction biplanes had become obsolete. (Open source)

A row of Tupolev SB-2 fast bombers. These examples are in Spanish service in 1940. These had been delivered by the Soviet Union to the Republicans before being captured by the Nationalists. They were then used in the Nationalists' own aviation. (Open source)

For reconnaissance, the IJAAC relied on the rugged, but highly reliable (and thus well-liked) Nakajima Ki-4, put into service in 1934. This versatile biplane was equipped with an air-cooled Nakajima Kotobuki Ha-8-I engine capable of developing 640hp on take-off. Intended for long-range flight, the aircraft was slow with a maximum speed of 283km/h at 2,400 metres. Its versatility could be seen through its nimbleness and its ability to conduct light bombing missions. Equipped with two Type 89 fixed machine guns firing through the propeller,

An R-5 in flight. This type, and several of its variants, were an essential part of the VVS during the 1930s, and were used as reconnaissance, light bomber and assault aircraft. (Open source)

a twin Type 89 was mounted on a flexible carriage for defensive purposes. A much more remarkable machine was the Ki-15. Developed by Mitsubishi following an IJAAC request in 1935 for a strategic reconnaissance aircraft capable of attaining 450km/h at 3,000 metres as well as being able to strike objectives 500 kilometres away from base, the prototype produced by Mitsubishi exceeded these requirements and was selected for use by the Japanese Army in 1937.

The first version of this aircraft, the Ki-15-I, was fitted with the same engine as the Ki-4 but it was capable of a maximum speed of 480km/h at 4,000 metres, and a range of 1,600 kilometres. Its main protection from enemy intercepts was its speed and it carried only a single 7.7mm machine gun for defensive purposes. Lastly, in 1938 the IJAAC introduced a small observation and liaison monoplane, the Tachikawa Ki-36. This also proved to be a reliable and sturdy machine able to operate from even the most testing air strips while being perfectly able to carry out its duties. Armed with two 7.7mm machine guns, one fixed while the second was placed on a flexible mount.

Both the Ki-4 and the Ki-36 were capable of carrying around 150kg of bombs and, therefore, able to conduct light attack missions. The IJAAC relied mostly on its light- and heavy bombers for offensive missions. By 1939, there were two types of very similar light bombers in service with the main difference between them being their weight-carrying capacity. Mitsubishi and Kawasaki both developed prototypes from 1936 in response to a request for a new

light bomber to replace both the Ki-3 and Ki-4. The requirements for the new aircraft were that it should be able to reach a speed of at least 400km/h and be capable of carrying from 300 to 450kg of bombs. The two companies both came up with fixed-carriage aircraft equipped with a bomb bay and able to carry 450kg of bombs, and both were armed with one fixed and one flexible-mounted 7.7mm machine gun. The top speeds of these aircraft were slightly superior at 420km/h, and each plane had a similar range. The Japanese Army commissioned the Mitsubishi Ki-30, propelled by a 1,000hp Nakajima Ha-5 Kai engine, in 1937. The Ki-32 had to wait another year to be accepted for use because its liquid-cooled Kawasaki Ha-9-II engine proved unreliable leading to a delay. If the cost of fielding two distinct aircraft for the same purpose seemed a high price to pay, Japanese requirements for aircraft were also high and by the end of 1939 it acquired 484 Ki-30s along with 694 Ki-32s. There had been production problems along the way, but more complicated concerns appeared when the IJAAC issued a call for heavy bombers.

The Mitsubishi Ki-1, in service since 1933, had performed disappointingly in China and in February 1936 the IJAAC launched an appeal to replace it. The requirements of its Air Bureau were challenging as the replacement was expected to be able to reach 400km/h, carry one ton of bombs and fly five-hour missions. Mitsubishi, the most experienced Japanese heavy bomber designer, struggled to satisfy these specifications. It was only in September 1937 that the Mitsubishi-designed Ki-21 was accepted and commissioned by the Japanese Army. Once in service, the new heavy

The R-10 was due to replace the R-5 but proved to be a disappointment. (Open source)

controlled seven Sentai. Of the seven, three were fighter units, two were heavy bombers units, one a reconnaissance unit and the last, a mixed reconnaissance and light bomber unit with a total of 77 fighters, 25 reconnaissance aircraft, 24 heavy bombers and six light bombers. If needed, reinforcements could be swiftly drawn from the 2nd Hiko Dan based in Korea and led by Lieutenant General Ebashi Eijiro. It included the 9th Sentai (30 Ki-10) and the 6th and 65th Sentai that had 28 Ki-32s between them. Crucially, most of the 2nd Hiko Shidan pilots were well experienced with 70 percent of them having 1,000 flight hours or more in their logbooks. There were also numerous combat veterans having served in China in the past.[12]

bomber proved to be a good aircraft with a range of 2,700 kilometres and top speed of 432km/h at 4,000 metres. This performance was produced by two Ha-5 Kai engines, the aircraft had a crew of seven airmen, carried six 7.7mm machine guns and one ton of bombs. 152 Ki-21s were produced in 1938 and 208 in 1939. The delay in producing the Ki-21 did, however, cause the Japanese military attaché in Rome, Lieutenant Colonel Seizo Arisue to contact the local authorities and to enquire about terms for the sale of 1,000 Fiat BR.20 bombers in six months. However, Tokyo would only approve the purchase of a single bomber for testing purposes, a decision that incensed the military attaché. Contacting high-ranking friends in the IJA, he convinced them to order 72 BR.20s. These were delivered in six batches of 12 aircraft beginning from January 1938 on. Soon renamed the 'heavy bomber Type I' (the I for Italy), the Fiats served with the 12th and 98th Sentai.[11]

The 2nd Air Division

In the aftermath of the Manchurian Incident, the IJAAC decided to create an air command directly attached to the Kwantung Army. By August 1932, the newly raised *Kantogun Hikotai* (Kwantung Army Flying Unit) included three daitai, and nine chutai with a total of around 100 aircraft. The build-up of this command corresponded to that of the Kwantung Army and by 1938 the rebaptised *Kantogun Hiko Shidan* (Kwantung Army Flying Division) had roughly 200 aircraft operated by five different *Hiko Rentai* as detailed in Table 9. After the reorganisation in 1938, this unit became the 2nd Hiko Shidan (2nd Air Division), and, by May 1939, the division oversaw the activities of the 7th, 9th and 12th Hiko Dan which, itself,

Winged Colossus

The *Voenno-Vozdushnye Sily RKKA* (Military Air Forces, or VVS) found its origin in its imperial forbearer. By December 1917, the latter had a total of 579 aircraft available with another 1,500 in storage, being overhauled or used for training. The Russian aviation did not have enough aircrew due to a lack of training facilities and local industry was unable to produce enough airframes and engines to sustain it. This made Russian aviation highly dependent on deliveries from allied countries. The Russian Civil War led to the disbandment of the service, and its personnel rallied either to the White factions or to the Bolsheviks, while some simply left the service and returned home. The next year, the Bolsheviks managed to create a total of 33 flights with six aircraft each, and these were overseen by the *Aviadarm* (Field Administration of Aviation Units) created in August 1918. By 1st February 1919, the nascent air branch had a total availability of 1,100 machines. However, for one reason or another, 719 of these were inoperable, as were some 300 aircrew, most of whom had been hastily trained. Because of the immense expanses over which the war was fought, and because of the tiny number of aircraft on hand at any given time, the young VVS learned to concentrate its available assets on crucial fronts, even if this meant leaving other fronts completely devoid of air cover. The bulk of the missions were reconnaissance and the VVS still managed to fly a total of 19,377 sorties dropping 94.5 tons of bombs in the process. It lost at least 473 aircraft; 83 in combat and the rest in accidents. Air combat was rare, and the VVS pilots claimed a total of 21 victories.

Once the war ended in 1923, the Soviet air force was in a pitiful state, operating a wide array of different aircraft types and the existing squadrons and flights being badly understrength. From 1924 the VVS underwent a restructuration with the

Table 12: 2nd Hiko Shidan, early May 1939	
2nd Hiko Shidan	**HQ in Hskinking. CO Lieutenant General Giga Testsuji**
7th Hiko Dan	**HQ in Kungchuling. CO Major General Hozoki Hisao**
1st Sentai	23 Ki-27
12th Sentai	12 BR.20
15th Sentai	9 Ki-4, 6 Ki-36, 4 Ki-15
9th Hiko Dan	**HQ in Tstishar. CO Major General Hikkaku Shimono**
10th Sentai	Mixed unit. One chutai with 9 Ki-30 and another with 6 Ki-15s
61st Sentai	12 Ki-21
12th Hiko Dan	**HQ in Harbin. CO Major General Higashi Eiji**
11th Sentai	36 Ki-27
24th Sentai	19 Ki-27

emphasis placed on recruiting and training the specialists needed to fill its existing order of battle. Nonetheless, the most enduring bottleneck remained the local aircraft industry which was lacking both in technological and production capabilities. Effectively, only 23 aircraft were produced in 1922-1923 while in 1923-1924 this figure rose to 264. Most were fitted with imported engines.

The restructuring led to the creation of a rather complex system with a combat branch being divided into two main components, the 'strategic' and the 'corps' aviation. The 'strategic' part included fighter, assault, bomber and reconnaissance squadrons while the mission of the second was to coordinate with the army during operations. Both were supported by a 'rear' branch in charge of the running of airfields, repair workshops, training facilities, research institutes and a miscellany of other departments or units. By 1928, the VVS had a total of 914 largely outdated aircraft (the main fighter remaining the locally produced variant of the Fokker D-XI). 532 of these were reconnaissance and liaison aircraft, 176 fighters, 168 bombers or attack aircraft and 26 trainers. This situation began to change at the end of the 1920s, especially as the aircraft industry became a focus of the first Five-Year Plan. Aircraft production began to rise significantly from 644 aircraft in 1927-1928 to 924 for 1928-1929. Another 5,109 aircraft left the factories between 1930 and 1932 allowing for a doubling in size of the VVS. By 1932 it disposed of 2,097 machines including 1,135 light bombers, attack, and reconnaissance aircraft, 487 fighters and 330 heavy bombers.

The Soviets encountered innumerable problems in the development of new technology. Indeed, Soviet factories suffered from endemic quality control issues and this led to an appeal for foreign expertise. Foreign specialists helped the Soviets to modernise and expand factories to the point that, by the mid-1930s (right in the middle of the second Five-Year Plan) there were four engine factories and 10 aircraft factories. These proved capable of churning out a staggering 4,270 aircraft and 11,326 engines in 1936. Quality control remained an issue especially as the immense pressure to produce ever more did not tempt factories to give this crucial aspect the attention it deserved. Even in 1936, entire batches of brand-new aircraft were almost unusable. To take one example, a batch of 62 I-16s delivered to Spain May 1937 had poorly manufactured engines and the wings of the aircraft had not been sufficiently strengthened. This led local Soviet advisers to report back to the 'Motherland' their belief that the aircraft had been "sabotaged."[13]

Cooperation with an array of German, French, British or US firms (licence agreements for aircraft engines, or specialist training) allowed for a major transfer of knowhow and enabled various Soviet aeronautic design bureaus to create aircraft whose performance was equivalent, or superior to, aircraft produced abroad. The design in 1930 of the I-5 biplane fighter by engineer Nikolai Polikarpov – the father of almost all Soviet fighters of the 1930s – was a watermark in this regard. By January 1937, the VVS had become a colossus with a fleet of 8,139 combat aircraft. Roughly 50 percent were heavy and light bombers, 30 percent were fighters and 20 percent were reconnaissance aircraft. The aircraft were assigned to *Aviapolk* (Air Regiments) that constituted the basic tactical units. Generally made up of several squadrons using a single type of aircraft, these units were overseen by *Aviabrigada* (Air Brigades). By 1938, the VVS had raised three *Armiya Osobogo Naznachiya* (AON), or Special Purpose Armies, that controlled two or three brigades, each composed of two regiments of heavy bombers (a total of 900 aircraft). Another peculiarity of the VVS was the emphasis placed on raising large numbers of assault, or *Shturmovaya* (Storm) units. By 1939, the *Istrebitelnyi Aviapolk* (IAP), or fighter regiment, had a

nominal strength of four squadrons with 15 aircraft each plus three aircraft that formed a regimental staff flight. The *Bombardirovochnyi Aviapolk* (BAP, or bomber regiment) possessed five squadrons of 12 aircraft plus a two-aircraft regimental staff flight.[14]

Red Doctrine

Towards the end of the 1920s, the VVS had developed a doctrine roughly similar to that of the IJAAC. The purpose of the air force was to gain aerial superiority in important areas around the front-line using a combination of aerial combat and air strikes against enemy air bases as a prerequisite to accomplishing its main mission: supporting ground forces. Therefore, the air force had a very tactical vocation right from the start. This is not to say that theoreticians such as the Italian Giulio Douhet did not have advocates in the Soviet Union. On the contrary, the VVS developed its own long-range bomber units with the intent of conducting what the Soviets called "independent air operations"; that is strategic bombing raids targeting enemy main cities and industries. In 1936, this led to the creation of an independent command devoted to this area. Much greater emphasis continued to be placed on supporting ground forces, nevertheless, and the VVS intended to play a crucial role in the 'Deep Battle' and 'Deep Operations' that had become the pilar of Soviet operational strategy by the mid-1930s. Indeed, as defined by the 1936 RKKA Field Regulations (Polevoi Ustav RKKA 1936; PU-36):

> As well as carrying out independent operations, air forces are to act in close conjunction with all-arm formations at operational and tactical levels. They are to undertake missions against enemy columns, troop concentrations and support elements (ground-attack aircraft and light bombers), bridges (bombers), and enemy aircraft and airfields (fighters, ground-attack aircraft, light bombers). They will also provide cover for friendly forces and dispositions.[15]

The significant involvement of the VVS in both Spain and China brought invaluable experience. It became evident that bombers were vulnerable to fighters, and so unescorted raids were to be avoided. China had shown that it was easier to defend large air bases far from the frontlines rather than bases located closer. Experience also demonstrated that the efficiency of enemy air raids against these bases could be largely diminished using camouflage, dispersal and anti-aircraft artillery. A series of engagements in Spain validated the ability of air support to influence the outcome of ground battles, while battles fought in both Spain and China validated the principle of concentrating assets for specific operations to gain potency. Soviet involvement in these wars also allowed pilots to gain combat experience against first-class adversaries. 160 pilots took part in the war in Spain between 1936 and 1939, and several hundred more served in China between 1937 and 1939. This infused units based in the USSR with a great deal of experience.

The Achilles' heel of the VVS remained the low number of flying hours given to pilots with an average of 70 hours per year. This was aggravated by the fact that a number of Soviet combat aircraft were comparatively difficult to master, and pilots needed time before being able to get the most out of their mounts. To add insult to injury, unit commanders tended to limit the time devoted to training out of the fear that too many aircraft would be lost in accidents as this had potentially deadly consequences in the Stalinist system. Much worse was to come in 1937. When the purges began in 1937, 4,724 out of the 13,000 officers serving in the VVS and the

PVO (air defence) were affected. These purges threw the Air Force into disarray and forced it to promote inexperienced or ill-qualified candidates to fill the gaps.[16]

Of gulls …

The mainstay of the VVS fighter arm from the mid-1930s were two aircraft developed simultaneously by the Polikarpov Design Bureau in 1933. The I-15 and the I-16 both used a mixture of metal and wood construction, and both were further improved in the following years giving birth to a series of variants. The I-15 was a biplane designed with manoeuvrability in mind, and its upper-wing had a gull-shape profile to lower aerodynamic resistance. This gave it the nickname 'Chaika', or 'seagull'. The prototype powered with a 480hp M-22 engine proved extremely promising as it enabled the aircraft to make a 360-degree turn in eight seconds and reach a maximum speed of 370km/h. A decision was taken to mass produce the aircraft and equip it with a 625hp M-25 engine. The first models being delivered to the VVS at the end of 1934, frontline units soon encountered endless problems related not only to numerous defects caused by the industry's lack of quality control and use of poor materials, but also inherent to the very design of the aircraft. More specifically, the M-25 engine mounting did not have a damper thus it generated a high level of vibrations that put stress on the airframe. Already lacking in strength, the I-15's gull wing induced a loss of longitudinal stability at speeds over 250km/h. The controls proved over-sensitive too, thus complicating the task of the pilots. The problems led to the discontinuation of the I-15 in 1935. However, they did not prevent the Soviets from shipping a total of 116 I-15s to Spain between October 1936 and May 1937. Here, by February 1937, 73 I-15s were being used by four squadrons of 57 pilots including 28 Soviets. Their first aerial combat occurred on 4 November 1936 when they shot down two Junkers Ju-52s. Despite its numerous flaws, the I-15 proved a match for fighters such as the Fiat CR.32 and the Heinkel He.51.

In the meantime, Polikarpov and his team of designers had been working on a second version of the I-15 since 1935 to address the most important defaults of the aircraft. This work led to the I-152 or I-15bis, an aircraft that entered production in mid-1937. The I-15bis kept the same armament of four PV-1 7.62mm machine guns, but it had a straight upper-wing instead of the gull wing. Its frame was reinforced, and it was powered by an M-25V engine with an output 20 percent superior to the M-25. Generating 775hp on take-off, this was, however, insufficient to compensate for the increase in weight prompted by the modifications. It also turned out that the I-15bis had a lower rate of climb, needing 6.6 minutes to reach 5,000 metres, and that while its top speed was similar to that of its predecessor, it was less manoeuvrable. After a series of mock air combats against the I-16, in September 1937 the VVS Scientific Research Institute concluded that the value of the aircraft was questionable: "In the environment of aerial combat the I-15 had no advantages over the I-16. All the advantages lie with the I-16. The I-15 is somewhat better from the standpoint of time-to-climb and manoeuvrability, while its only by virtue of the M-25V engine's power reserves that the I-15 can break away from combat is by diving."[17]

This did not prevent the VVS from sticking to its doctrine of equipping its fighter units with both biplane and monoplane fighters, the intention of which was to combine the manoeuvrability of the former with the speed of the latter. In this respect, production of the I-15bis not only continued until 1939 resulting in the building of 2,408 I-15bis, but Polikarpov began to work on a third version of the fighter in 1937. Also incorporating the lessons drawn from the

Spanish theatre, the first prototypes of the I-153 were completed in the autumn of the same year.

The frame of the aircraft was strengthened even further, and the upper gull-shaped wing reintroduced. The aircraft was powered by a 1,100hp M-62 engine and equipped with retractable landing gear. This allowed the I-153 to reach a maximum speed at 5,000 metres while it needed 5.7 minutes to reach this altitude. It could also complete a 360-degree turn in 13.5 seconds and the weaponry was improved with the fitting of four synchronised ShKAS 7.62mm machine guns. The *Shpitalny-Komaritski Aviatsionny Skorostreink* (Shpitalny-Komaritski rapid-firing machine gun) was a unique weapon for its time and could fire 1,800 rounds per minute. It was a comparatively light machine gun a fighter equipped with four of these weapons could fire as many as 120 rounds, or 1.43kg of ammunition, per second. The first prototype flew in 1938 with production beginning in early 1939, although problems with both the M-62 engine and the variable-pitch propeller delayed its official introduction in the VVS. Still, a limited number of I-153s were ready to take part in the Nomonhan Incident, but their participation only confirmed that biplane fighters were becoming obsolete. In the words of Major Stepan Danilov: "We had problems with our *chaikas*. They were certainly fewer than with the I-15bis, but we still had problems. We had no speed, and no manoeuvre is helped when you have no speed. Spin as much you like. They will still attack you from above".[18]

… and donkeys

The VVS's main monoplane fighter proved more satisfactory, but far from being trouble free. The I-16 first prototype, powered with an M-22 engine, first flew in the end of 1933. The new fighter incorporated an array of very innovative features such as its enclosed cockpit and its retractable landing gear. It also had a strong frame despite it consisting mostly of plywood covered with canvas, and metal tubing being used in the tail. A positive note was that this allowed for good diving speeds. The I-16 being fast and comparatively manoeuvrable, these assets did, however, come at a price. Effectively, increased manoeuvrability was gained by placing the centre of gravity aft, but it also made it unforgiving and difficult to master. Even the most experienced pilots found that it lacked stability and that its landing speed was too high. More than half the losses of the I-16 in Spain were caused by accidents relating to these issues earning the aircraft the nickname 'Ishak', or donkey. Still equipped with the M-22 engine, the new aircraft entered production in 1934 and became known as the Type 4. A Type 5 came into being in 1936, and this model was essentially the same aircraft, the main difference was its M-25 engine that allowed it to reach a top speed of 445kmh. This was the version that was used by the USSR in Spain. A first batch of 31 I-16 Type 5s and 31 pilots arrived in Spain in early November 1936. Followed by five squadrons of I-16s a year later, by mid-1937 they were completely outmatching the enemy CR.32s and He.51s enabling Republican forces to gain, and to maintain air superiority, which did not change until the appearance of the early versions of the Bf.109. When they did arrive, they allowed the Nationalists to gradually turn the tables on the Republicans. The appearance of the Bf.109 only served to encourage Soviet authorities to improve the I-16. The new variant was called the Type 10, and the version produced in 1938 was equipped with an M-25V engine and a variable-pitch propeller bringing its top speed to 448km/h. It also had a strengthened armament with four ShKAS machine guns instead of the previous two. The pilot was also now better protected as an 8mm armoured plate was fitted behind the seat of the cockpit.

Next came the Type 17. This version of the I-16 was much more powerful in terms of firepower than its predecessors. Two ShVAK 20mm cannons were placed in the wings, but the aircraft could now reach a top speed of only 425km/h with a rate of climb at 882 metres per minute. On the other hand, the potency of the Type 10 and Type 17's firepower was partially cancelled out by the aircraft's instability, which made it a poor firing platform. Another development was the Type 18. It was similar in many ways to the Type 10, but it was powered by an M-62 engine that could reach a maximum speed of 464km/h while enabling a climb rate of 1,034 metres per minute. The I-15bis, the I-153 and the I-16 having been produced in large numbers – 1,304 I-15bis, 1,011

A Nakajima Ki-27, or Army Fighter Type 97, of the 24th Sentai. (Albert Grandolini Collection)

I-153s and 1,147 I-16s in 1939 alone – in mid-September 1939, the VVS IAP consisted of 2,501 I-16s, 1,647 I-15bis and 160 I-153s.

The Soviets and the Japanese were, in theory, more than aware of the strengths of their respective opponents. The USSR not only sent 216 Type 5s and 10s and 347 I-15bis to China between October 1937 and September 1939, but it also sent hundreds of fighter pilots. Engaged in countless air combats during this period, the pilots were presented with ample opportunity to assess the capabilities of the Japanese Ki-10 and Ki-27 fighters and the skills of their pilots. Naturally, the Japanese were also able to weigh up the strength of the Soviets. An example of this mutual scrutiny can be seen through encounters with the Ki-27. Indeed, the VVS fighter pilots could not have helped noticing that they were at a disadvantage, as while the Japanese aircraft were fitted with radio transmitters or receivers, the Soviets were still using hand signals.[19]

Tupolevs and Polikarpovs

The VVS adopted an increasingly offensive attitude in the 1930s and the Tupolev Design Bureau soon became tasked with developing a dedicated *Skorostnoy Bombardirovshchik* (SB), or fast bomber. A first prototype of the SB-2 flew on 30 December 1934, and while the design proved promising enough it took another year to further hone the aircraft. This was done by equipping it with two 860hp M-100 water-cooled engines. Once it entered production at the end of 1935, the SB-2 was an impressive aircraft able to fly at a maximum speed of 423km/h while carrying a normal load of 600kg of bombs over 1,600 kilometres. This all-metal monoplane carried a crew of three as well as three ShKAS machine guns for defensive purposes, and its sheer speed made it difficult to intercept. This was so even after the appearance of the Ki-27 in China which forced the SB to fly at higher altitudes. The role of the crew was complicated by the small and uncomfortable sitting positions within the cockpit that partially blocked their view. Another problem was the aircraft lacked protection. This was addressed through the designing of the SB-2bis which, moreover, was fitted with two 960hp M-103 engines allowing

it to reach a top speed of 450km/h. The frame of the aircraft was strengthened enabling it to carry 1,500kgs of bombs, but a drawback was that this extra weight radically decreased the range and speed of the aircraft compared to when it carried its normal load of 600kg. Another Tupolev design was the massive TB-3 heavy bomber. Plans were drawn up in 1929 and production began in 1932, by 1939 this four-engined aircraft had become obsolete. The VVS used it for night missions only, it was here that its ability to drop three tons of bombs could be put to good use without exposing it to enemy fighters otherwise able to make short work of the giant, but relatively slow-paced, bomber.

A shortcoming of the VVS that became apparent in 1939 was the obsolescence of its reconnaissance and attack aircraft. The mainstay of its related fleet remained the Polikarpov R-5, but this reconnaissance aircraft doubling as a light bomber had entered production in 1929. A two-seat biplane, it was powered by a 680hp water-cooled M-17B engine and could reach a top speed of 244km/h. As for its weaponry, it was armed with a single fixed forward firing PV-1 7.62mm machine gun and a twin flexible-mounted PV-1 machine gun for defensive purpose and could carry 400kg of bombs. In 1934, the aircraft became the R-5SSS and was fitted with a 715hp M-17F engine and ShKAS machine guns. It could carry 500kgs of bombs and its maximum speed increased to 249km/h. A much-improved version known as the R-Z was developed the following year. It had a new monocoque fuselage, a semi-enclosed cockpit, reduced wing surface and a liquid-cooled 850hp M-34RN engine. The R-Z could reach a top speed of 316km/h but, otherwise, its weaponry was similar to its predecessors. A total of 4,914 R-5s, 620 R-5SSSs and 1,031 R-Zs were produced between 1929 and 1939. In 1934, engineer Iosif Nyeman began to work on a replacement for the R-5, and this led to the appearance of the R-10. Another monoplane equipped with a bomb bay, a retractable undercarriage and powered by a M-25B engine, this aircraft entered service in 1937 but it disappointed due to its maximum speed of 370km/h. By the end of 1938 and the arrest of Nyeman, only 100 R-10s had

A group of officers pose in front of the remains of a SB-2. (Albert Grandolini Collection)

been produced. All these designs were outclassed by their Japanese counterparts such as the Ki-30 and Ki-32 and were horrendously vulnerable to enemy fighters. Predictably, the Soviets limited their use to a supporting role during the incident and, instead, deployed fighters for reconnaissance or assault purposes. Here, the I-16 Type 17 proved itself especially deadly thanks to its two 20mm guns.[20]

Comrade Feklenko's Air Force

As with anything related to the small-sized Mongolian People's Army, the Soviets played an instrumental role in the growth of its fledgling air component. By the end of 1938, it had limited resources with a total of 45 R-5s and 27 mostly inexperienced pilots assigned to two regiments. The 1st Ground Attack Regiment flew 17 R-5Shs

while the 2nd Light Bomber Regiment had 19 R-5s at its disposal. As a result, the bulk of air assets available in Mongolia corresponded to the VVS 100th *Smeshannaya Aviabrigada* (Mixed Brigade; SABR) which was deployed in the country together with the 57th KON. Consequently, the mixed air brigade, was nicknamed 'Comrade Feklenko's Air Force'. Mid-May 1939 saw the 100th SABR led by Lt Colonel Viktor Yefimovich Nyestyertsyev and composed of two regiments. The 70th IAP (CO Major Vyacheslav Zabaluyev) had 39 I-16 Type 5s and I-15bis at its service, while the 150th *Smeshennyi Bombardirovochnyi Aviapolk* (SBAP) (or mixed bomber regiment) under Major

Mikhael Burmistrov disposed of five squadrons and a total of 36 SB-2 fast bombers and 17 R-5Shs. Despite appearances, this force was much less impressive that it seemed. Firstly, many aircraft were worn out and only nine out of the 14 I-15bis and 13 out of the 24 I-16s of the 70th IAP were airworthy. Aircrew morale tended to be low, as being assigned to Mongolia was akin to being left in the desert. On average, nearly 60 percent of the pilots had either departed on leave or were on sick leave. Most were very inexperienced having only between 60 to 120 flight hours in their logbooks. Another point to consider was that the 150th SBAP was still in the process of converting to the SB-2, it being delivered to the unit only on 1 May 1939. It would be true to say that the 100th SABR could hardly be considered as combat-ready.[21]

5

IN THE ENDLESS SKIES

Following the first skirmishes in the Nomonhan area in early May 1939, the Kwantung Army sent to Hailar to support the Azuma Detachment a *Rinji Hikotai* (temporary air unit) made up of one chutai of six Ki-30s from the 10th Sentai, and two chutai of the 24th Sentai with 19 Ki-27s. Joining these units were the 48th and 51st Airfield battalions whose role was to build airstrips and the necessary infrastructure. On 15 May, five Ki-30s bombed a Mongolian outpost and three days later, groups of three fighters from the 24th Sentai began to patrol the same sector. It was not long before this activity triggered a series of clashes against aircraft of the 100th SABR. On 20 May, a Japanese plane reported that it had sighted an R-5 and had shot it down.[1] On the following day, another Japanese patrol sighted and shot down an R-5, killing the pilot, and other Ki-27 pilots reported having encountered a trio of I-15bis. On 22 May, a mixed formation of three I-15bis and two I-16s from the 70th IAP was attacked by three Japanese fighters. One I-16 was shot down and the pilot killed. These encounters proved enough to persuade

both sides to rush reinforcements to the area. On 23 May, the 12th Hiko Dan, two chutai of the 11th Sentai (20 Ki-27s), a chutai of the 10th Sentai (six K-15s), the 22nd Airfield Battalion and the 2nd Air Intelligence Unit were ordered to Hailar. Concurrently, the Trans-Baikal Military District ordered the 23rd SABR to move to Tamsag Bulak. The 23rd SABR included the 22nd IAP (CO Major Nikolay Glazikin) and the 38th SBAP (CO Captain Vladirmir Artamonov), with the former arriving in Tamsag-Bulak on 26 May, followed a few days later by the 59 SB-2s of the latter. The 22nd IAP was at full strength with 63 aircraft including 35 I-15bis and 28 I-16 Type 10s. On the other hand, its pilots were as ill-trained as those from 70th IAP, the commander of the 23rd SABR noting that "Airmen from the 22nd IAP have been reluctant to fly for fear of crashing when they should have been improving their flying skills and practising attacks in groups."[2]

The reinforcements allowed the Soviets to withdraw the 70th IAP from the area to be re-equipped with new machines and aerial combat further increased over the coming days. Events started on 27 May, when the 22nd IAP moved forward eight I-16 Type 10s to a crude airstrip close to the Halha River. Shortly, three Nakajimas of the 11th Sentai overflew the airstrip prompting the Soviets to scramble six I-16s that climbed in pursuit of the enemy aircraft. It turned out to be a trap as two three-aircraft *shotai* lay in wait and scattered the Soviet formation shooting down three I-16s in quick succession and without loss. The following day proved even more eventful. After a chutai of the 11th Sentai shot down a patrol of three I-15bis from the 70th IAP killing their pilots, a formation of 10 I-15bis from the 22nd IAP was attacked by 18 Ki-27s. The slower VVS biplanes were virtually slaughtered with six shot-down and three others forced to make crash landings. In this incident, four Soviet pilots died, and two others were wounded. The 11th Sentai lost a fighter during the melee but its pilot, Lieutenant Sadayoshi Mitsutomi, managed to bail out. He was retrieved by another Ki-27. Significantly, the Japanese claimed 42 victories during these encounters, and in a matter of two days the Soviets had lost 15 fighters with 11 pilots killed in action. In return, they shot down a single Japanese fighter. Shocked by these figures, the VVS resisted challenging the Japanese for the next few days.[3]

VVS "Experten"

The heavy defeat suffered by the Azuma Regiment coincided with an IJAAC decision to suspend flights over the contested area. Consequently, Soviet reconnaissance planes crossing into Manchurian territory were free from attacks. The halt in fighting allowed the VVS to assess their failures and to conclude that the defeat in question was foremostly the result of the inexperience of its pilots, and a lack of training that led to errors of judgement being made. One such error was the decision to use formations of I-15bis that were not provided with support from I-16s. To address this issue, a core group of 22 veteran pilots from the Spanish and Chinese campaigns had been selected and assembled in Moscow, along with 26 similarly experienced navigators and engineers. On 29 May, they left the Soviet capital aboard three DC-3s and arrived in Mongolia on 4 June. The veterans were put in command of the fighter units and immediately set up a crash-course for inexperience pilots. The intention of the course being to improve the skills used in air combat, formations of combined units of I-15 and I-16 fighters were trained through the organisation of mock battles. Feedback on the battles was given so that the lessons learned could be applied to future encounters with the enemy, and the lost aircraft were replaced to bring the squadrons up to full strength. In the meantime, several pilots sourced from various bases and regiments in the USSR were sent to Mongolia on a tour of duty bringing the number of IAPs in the area to as many as seven squadrons. By 21 June, the 70th IAP disposed of 60 I-16s and 24 I-15bis, while the 22nd IAP had 35 I-16s (including the Type 17 squadron) and 32 I-15bis. As for the 38th and the 150th SBAP, these units consisted of 135 SB-2s and 15 R-5Shs between them. There were also another 35 R-5s operated by the two Mongolian regiments.[4]

The lull in fighting ended abruptly on 17 June when the VVS attacked several positions in Manchurian territory causing the Japanese to resume their operations. On 18 June, the 2nd Hiko Shidan was ordered to mass its units in Hailar to support an imminent ground offensive by the 23rd Division, and to intercept enemy fighters crossing the border. Before long, the entire 11th and 24th Sentai had been sent to the area along with the 1st Sentai, which included 23 Ki-27s and had been sent to Manchuria in early June. This brought the number of Japanese fighters to 77. The situation escalated considerably on 22 June when the Soviets dispatched a large formation of aircraft to attack Japanese forces on the eastern shore of the Halha River. The Japanese reacted by scrambling 18 Ki-27s of the 24th Sentai that made a sweep over the border but arrived too late to intercept the raiders. This prompted the 22nd IAP to dispatch one squadron of 12 I-16s and another of 10 I-15bis to intercept. However, the two units failed to coordinate and the faster I-16s arrived first on the scene. These aircraft were attacked by the Japanese who shot down the squadron leader throwing the unit into disarray. The other I-16 pilots swiftly disengaged. The 24th Sentai's pilots therefore found themselves in the perfect position to deal with the squadron of I-15bis and shot down three planes before other fighters of the 70th IAP could come to the rescue. These events were described by Captain Kani Saiji, the 1st Chutai leader of the 24th Sentai:

There were many enemy aircraft, but we had the courage of eagles pursuing swallows and overwhelmed the enemy. At around 17.30, I spotted 25-26 enemy aircraft at [an altitude of] 2,000 metres. The first pass brought one plane down in flames, and one by one, others followed. More new enemy aircraft appeared and entered the battle, and we were surrounded. We left the area and returned home. There were many hits to the wings and tail of my aircraft.[5]

The wreck of a shot down I-16 being inspected by Japanese soldiers. (Albert Grandolini Collection)

This photograph of Ki-27s from the 24th Sentai gives a good hint of what the battlefield airstrips looked like. As can be seen, they were little more than levelled areas of open plain. (Albert Grandolini Collection)

What happened next is that both sides continued to send their fighters over the Halha River. This set off a second large-scale and confused encounter, described in the following way by Arseniy Vorozheykin, the pilot of an I-16 attached to the 22nd IAP:

The squadron approached Khalkin Gol in compact order. High above us we saw a flight of Japanese fighters and Squadron Commander Captain Vasiliy Gugashin was determined to hunt down the enemy at any cost. He began chasing the Japanese at full throttle, leaving his wingman far behind. The formation became stretched and scattered. The enemy flight, however, had the advantage of height and escaped. My leader abandoned the chase and swerved away. Meanwhile, far away to the left of us was a large swarm of aircraft. At first, I thought they were our own fighters from the leading group but there were too many of them; around 60. There was also something strange in the way they flew. They advanced assuredly and precisely as if they believed themselves to be lords of the Mongolian sky. I tried to warn my commander by rocking my wings, but he wouldn't pay any attention. He was focused on another formation ahead of us that was almost certainly made up of friendly aircraft. He hadn't seen the Japanese machines, so with a few others I broke away from our commander's course to take on the real enemy. At that point I didn't see anything but the enemy fighters ahead.

Suddenly, an avalanche fell on the Japanese flight from somewhere above. The strike was powerful and unexpected to the extent that it seemed as if a tremendous explosion had scattered the enemy formation leaving burning aircraft behind. It was then that a 'mad dance' began. Although initially overwhelmed by the sudden attack, I quickly spotted more JAAF fighters coming to the rescue. We had to intercept them, so we hurried to meet the newcomers face-to-face attacking head-on. There would be no swerving away. Everything inside me tensed up like a string as I held my breath. But the number of enemy fighters grew all too quickly. Instinctively, I fired the machine gun without aiming, and streams of bullets shot out from the front of my fighter. Suddenly,

the Japanese aircraft were gone. I just couldn't believe it was all over.[6]

At day's end, the Japanese had lost seven Ki-27s with three pilots killed and another captured. The Japanese claimed 52 victories, while the Soviets claimed 31 with the loss of 13 I-15bis, one I-16 and 11 pilots killed. 105 of their aircraft took part in the two battles. Expectedly, both sides clashed again on 24 June during another three dogfights. The day ended with the loss of two I-15bis from the 70th IAP as well as one SB-2. The 11th Sentai lost one Ki-27. On 26 June, three squadrons made up of 27 I-16s and 13 I-15bis from the 70th IAP sighted two chutai of the 1st Sentai in the vicinity of the Halha River. The Japanese immediately turned east with the Soviets in hot pursuit, and they continued until the Soviets were ambushed by several chutai from the 11th and 24th Sentai that lay in wait around 70 kilometres away from the border. The Soviets had a lucky escape and soon they were joined by 41 I-15bis and I-16s from the 22nd IAP. The encounter ended in a clear victory for the Japanese: they suffered no losses while three I-16s and one I-15bis were shot down.[7]

At Dawn We Slept

The commander of the 2nd Hiko Shidan, Lieutenant General Giga, was anything but confident about the success of his fighter pilots. They were becoming increasingly tired by the ceaseless combat missions and Giga feared that his men would be exhausted if fighting continued indefinitely. On the other hand, the Soviets apparently benefitted from continual reinforcement. Indeed, by 19 June Japanese intelligence assessed that the VVS consisted of between 110 and 140 combat aircraft available in the area and that these numbers were rapidly increasing.

According to IJAAC doctrine, on the eve of the ground offensive there was only one method that could be used to deal a decisive blow to Soviet air power: an all-out attack against the VVS air bases around Tamsag Bulag. The belligerent Kwantung Army Staff gave its approval to this attack on 2 June, but it being opposed by the Army General Staff (see Chapter Three), the final preparations took place on 26 June when a Ki-15 overflew the main bases of the VVS and reported the presence of around 200 aircraft at Tamsag Bulag. The attack against Tamsag Bulag finally took place at dawn on 27 June, and it involved the 12 Fiat BR.20s from the 12th Sentai, nine Ki-21s and six Ki-30s provided by the 61st and 10th Sentai respectively, plus a dozen Ki-15s and almost all the Ki-27s that the 1st, 11th and 24th Sentai could send into the air. The 24th Sentai was to provide top cover for the entire formation, the 1st and 11th Sentai were to hunt for Soviet aircraft in the air or strafe the airfields. The attack took the Soviets completely by surprise meaning that their fighters had to be hastily scrambled once the first Japanese planes had dropped their bombs. As a result, several of them proved easy pickings for the 1st

A Japanese pilot of the 15th Sentai reports to 23rd Division officers. Despite the Ki-4 being well-liked by its crew, this aircraft had become obsolete by 1939. (Albert Grandolini Collection)

and 11th Sentai pilots. Once the air strike had been completed, the 2nd Hiko Shidan launched another attack against Bain Tumen but the small airfield almost devoid of enemy presence. Other strikes were cancelled the day after due to the furious reaction of the AGS. In total, 17 I-16s and I-15bis were shot down, killing at least six pilots. Another eight aircraft were destroyed on the ground. As for Japanese forces, they lost five aircraft including three fighters, one bomber and one reconnaissance aircraft. Seven pilots and crewmen were killed and another two wounded. Soviet anti-aircraft artillery proved accurate and damaged a third of the Japanese heavy bombers. As usual, the Japanese massively overestimated the losses they had inflicted claiming to have shot down 99 enemy aircraft and destroyed another 25 on the ground. The 2nd Air Division, therefore, ended the day concluding that it had gained a major victory whereas, in reality, much more would have been needed

to significantly impede the capability of the VVS to operate over the battlefields.[8] There were to be no further attacks against Soviet airfields for weeks after because of the reaction of the AGS. From 29 June, even fighter operations were limited to the eastern part of the Halha River.

Deadly Swarms

Naturally, the Japanese ground offensive in early July sparked off numerous encounters in the sky, especially from 2 July when both air forces sent out groups of bombers to strike enemy positions.

The bombers were invariably escorted by large groups of fighters generating a series of large-scale dogfights. The VVS used its so-called "air conveyor" tactic developed in Spain. Waves of heavily escorted bombers and fighters were sent one after the other leaving dazed and disorganised Japanese with the task of confronting a freshly arrived enemy again and again. In this respect, 3 July proved particularly intensive. At dawn, the Ki-30s of the 10th and 16th Sentai and the Ki-21s of the 61st Sentai launched a series of vicious attacks against the Mongolian 6th Cavalry Division positions on Bain Tsagan. To support the 23rd Division's crossing of the Halha River. Zhukov soon ordered the VVS to go all-out and to support his hastily organised counter-attack. Seventy-three SB-2s were sent to bomb Japanese positions around Bain Tsagan with the Soviet fast bomber squadrons following each other at 400-metre intervals. They were followed by other SB formations during the day, and attacks were focused on the Japanese bridge. Soviet fighters performed escort duties while I-16 Type 17s and I-15bis strafed Japanese anti-aircraft artillery and troop positions. As was to be expected, the day saw several large-scale dogfights, too. That day, the SB-2s dropped a total of 6,000 FAB-100 and FAB-250 bombs but lost three bombers. Additionally, an I-16 was shot down. Japanese losses, on the other hand, remain unclear. 4 and 5 July were, more or less, a repeat of 3 July, but they proved more costly for the VVS. It lost seven SB bombers on 4 July and another two the following day. The IJAAC acknowledged the loss of a single Ki-27 over these two days. Of note was the entry into combat of the brand-new I-153 on 4 July. The tempo of operations lessened on 6 July, with a single SB-2 being lost that day to anti-aircraft fire. This brought the total number of VVS aircraft shot down between 2 and 6 July to 16.[9]

Dogfights continued at a high pace until 12 July as the 23rd Division launched a series of night raids against the Soviet pocket on the eastern shore of the Halha River. The IJAAC claimed to have shot down 152 enemy aircraft from 8 to 12 July 1939 while admitting the loss of seven fighters. As always, VVS losses were much less spectacular. Effectively, the Japanese claimed 63 victories on 10 July in a series of air battles against the 22nd and 70th IAP losing a single Ki-27 in the process, whilst the Soviets lost three I-16s. After a 10-day lull in the fighting, large-scale engagements were resumed on 21 July when the IJAAC flew the first of a series of bombing raids in preparation

An unsung part of the quest for air supremacy. Both sides mobilised comparatively high numbers of anti-aircraft guns, cannons, and machine guns, such as this Soviet quadruple Maxim M1910/30. (Albert Grandolini Collection)

A group of VVS fighter pilots taking a break in front of their I-16. Initially much less experienced than their Japanese counterparts, they followed a steep learning curve from June to August. (Albert Grandolini Collection)

The VVS "Experten" sent to beef-up the embattled units in Mongolia travelled aboard DC-3s such as this one. Along with aircraft such as the TB-3, DC-3s were used extensively to carry supplies and evacuate wounded from the battlefield. (Albert Grandolini Collection)

a single Ki-30 and four Ki-27s that day. Fighting continued until 27 July when the weather did not permit large-scale air operations for a few days.[10]

Reinforcements

By 3 July, the VVS and Mongolian units supporting the 1st Army Group had a total of 138 I-15bis and I-16 fighters, plus 135 SB-2 bombers and 35 R-5s. Already numerically superior to their Japanese opponents, the Soviets were determined to gain superiority in the air, though their intelligence wildly overestimated the strength of the 2nd Hiko Shidan. As a result of this overestimation of the number of enemy planes, Soviet reinforcements continued to flow towards the battle area throughout July and August 1939. Both the 56th IAP and the 56th SBAP arrived during July, as did two TB-3 squadrons from the 4th TBAP (Heavy Bomber Air Regiment), which flew night raids against Japanese positions. By early August, the VVS inventory had risen to 532 aircraft. This included 194 I-16s (mostly Type 10 and 17), 70 I-153s, 57 I-15bis and 181 SB-2s. The command structure was also simplified with all the bomber regiments being regrouped into a single entity, the 100th SBAB. At the same time, a fighter command oversaw the activities of the 22nd, 56th and 70th IAP. On top of this, several other units including the 8th and 32nd IAP, and the 49th SBAP were kept battle-ready in the Trans-Baikal Military District in case of a development in the Mongolian situation.

for a new ground offensive. The bombers were heavily escorted by aircraft from the 1st and 24th Sentai, and before long they were engaged by 97 I-15bis and 62 I-16s scrambled by the 22nd and 70th IAP. After a battle that lasted an hour and a half, five I-15bis and their pilots had been lost while the Japanese lost three fighters. On 23 July, the 2nd Hiko Shidan went all-out to support the start of the 23rd Division's artillery offensive, and the Ki-30s and Ki-21s of the 10th, 16th and 61st Sentai flew a total of 128 missions dropping 48 tons of bombs in the process. Several Ki-30 crews flew as many as three sorties that day. Naturally, the Soviets replied in kind and the SB-2s carried out eight distinct raids totalling at least 140 sorties between them. Soviet losses remain unclear, but the Japanese lost

As for the Japanese, the IJAAC struggled to reinforce the embattled 2nd Hiko Shidan. This was, mainly, because the war in China mobilised the bulk of its resources. The 12th Sentai and its BR.20 were withdrawn because of the increasing difficulty to keep the Italian bombers operational, and this was compensated with the arrival of the Ki-30-equipped 16th Sentai. By July's end, the 64th Sentai and its 33 Ki-27 fighters were ordered from China to Manchuria. The 7th Hiko Dan was disbanded, and its assets transferred to the 9th and 12th Hiko Dan. By early August, the Japanese air division included a total of two brigades and eight regiments totalling roughly 180 aircraft.[11]

Table 13: 2nd Hiko Shidan, Early August 1939	
2nd Hiko Shidan	HQ in Hskinking. CO Lieutenant General Giga Testsuji
15th Sentai	At least 10 Ki-15 and Ki-4
9th Hiko Dan	
10th Sentai	9 Ki-30, 5 Ki-36
16th Sentai	Around 20 Ki-30
61st Sentai	9 Ki-21
12th Hiko Dan	
1st Sentai	23 Ki-27
11th Sentai	42 Ki-27
24th Sentai	26 Ki-27
64th Sentai	33 Ki-27

Table 14: VVS 1st Army Group Order of Battle, mid-July 1939[12]
Fighter Component
22nd IAP
70th IAP
56th IAP
100th SBAB
150th SBAP
38th SBAP
56th SBAP
4th TBAP (detachment)

Striking the Nests

On 25 July, Moscow lifted the ban on penetrating Manchukuoan airspace. Soon, the VVS decided to seize the opportunity to increase pressure on its nemesis by introducing another tactic developed in Spain: the strafing of enemy airfields. From 27 July, pairs of fighter aircraft were sent into enemy territory to locate the Japanese forward airfields, and a first attack was launched at dawn on 29 July. Twenty-seven I-16s from the 22nd IAP attacked the Alay forward airfield at 0715 hours, a mere 12 kilometres from the border. The Soviet formation approached the target area from an altitude of 150 metres before splitting into two groups. Two squadrons including several I-16 Type 17s climbed to 2,000 metres before initiating a strafing run against the airfield. A third squadron climbed to 3,500 metres to provide top cover for the other two. The Soviets took the Japanese by surprise. Two Ki-27s from the 11th Sentai, 2nd Chutai were destroyed and another nine damaged on the ground. A second attack by a smaller formation a few hours later saw the I-16s surprise five Ki-27s that were preparing to land. Two were shot down, their pilots killed, and another two Japanese pilots were wounded during the encounter.

The next raid happened on 2 August at 0725 hours. Wrought in a similar fashion, this time 70th IAP fell on the Tchintching Sume Airfield, the home of the 15th Sentai. Twenty-three I-16s strafed the Japanese aircraft – which, incredibly, were not dispersed – and a dozen aircraft were reported to have been destroyed. When aircraft of the 70th IAP arrived, they shot down a single Ki-36 killing the CO of the 15th Sentai, Colonel Abe, in the process. The 2nd Hiko Shidan reacted by withdrawing its units from the airfields located close to the border. The result was that another raid on 4 August failed because the targeted airfield was empty. The Soviets had to send their strike formations deeper into Manchukuoan territory to reach their targets, and this gave the Japanese more time to detect them and scramble their fighters. On 5 August, a formation including 60 I-16s was intercepted by Ki-27s from the 1st and 11th Sentai. Two Ki-27s were lost during the engagement but the raid was aborted. A similar event occurred on 7 August when the 11th Sentai intercepted another 60 I-16s flying toward Hailar. One was shot down, but the Japanese lost one fighter in the process. The VVS launched several other strafing attacks against airfields in the coming days, and on 19 August I-16s destroyed a 64th Sentai Ki-27 on the ground. Despite the Soviet's kill-rate remaining low, their "Airfield Blitz" succeeded in hindering enemy operations because the Japanese had to operate from bases further away from the front and had to disperse their aircraft accordingly. The 2nd Hiko Shidan requested approval from Tokyo to reply in kind, and it was authorised to do so on 7 August. However, adverse weather and exhaustion forced the unit to postpone any new large-scale attack until the August Soviet offensive.[13]

The Spectre of Attrition

As had been predicted in June, the Japanese were fighting a downhill battle. Their fighter

The Japanese were not alone when it came to inspecting enemy wrecks. Here, RKKA soldiers examine the remains of a shot down Ki-21. (Albert Grandolini Collection)

A row of Ki-27s from the 64th Sentai. While the unit arrived late during the incident, it suffered heavily if only because it found itself on the receiving end of one the deadly VVS strafing attacks. (Open source)

pilots had exhausted themselves by flying repeated patrols over contested areas for several weeks logging as many as seven missions per day. The effect of frequent, large-scale, air combats gradually thinning their ranks, the pilots killed were usually unit commanders or aces, weakening the air units even further. Naturally, the aircraft themselves were affected through their intensive use and frequent

damage caused by enemy fire. To make the situation worse, the IJAAC was unable to implement a rotation system, and insisted on the need for the Sentai to remain in the theatre for weeks on end. The collective effect was to render missions almost suicidal, and to leave Japanese aircraft open to attack from Soviet fighters roaming over the area. Slowly, but surely, the IJAAC was losing the fight against the VVS. The conflict was not just a quantitative struggle, however. Soviet pilots were as committed to the fight as their Japanese counterparts, and from time-to-time pilots from both sides attempted to ram an opponent when they had run out of ammunition or had been badly wounded. The Soviets also improved their flying strategy by gradually withdrawing vulnerable I-15s which more often than not, had been purposely targeted by Japanese pilots who had identified them as easy prey, and used instead I-16s and I-153s. The main weakness of the Ki-27, that is its inability to sustain high-speed dives, was identified by the VVS pilots which soon enough adopted the "Boom and Zoom" or "Energy Tactics", thus avoiding close-quarter, manoeuvring dogfights by flying at high altitude, dive, briefly fire on their targets and climb again to repeat the entire process. To make matters worse, Soviet fighters flew in formations called "three layers" by the Japanese with groups flying simultaneously at low, medium and high altitude, thus guaranteeing

A Soviet officer proudly poses with a wrecked Ki-27 from the 11th Sentai. (Albert Grandolini Collection)

Personnel of the 11th Sentai eating their lunch before a new round of sorties. (Albert Grandolini Collection)

A rare picture of a Ki-30 light bomber flying over the Halha River. (Albert Grandolini Collection)

A Japanese officer posing in front of a captured I-16 after it had been made to carry out a forced landing. (Albert Grandolini Collection)

would have done. But, if we sortied with the whole wing of four groups, as we often did, the foe stayed away from us, so we used the wing to retain air superiority and encourage the ground forces.[14]

As for problems, the VVS had its fair share. The number of SB-2s lost demonstrated that they were highly vulnerable to enemy fighters, the main reason being that there was only one crewman for both the upper and lower machine gun positions. Although this issue was overcome by SBAP bombers increasing their flying height from 3,000 to between 6,500 and 7,000 metres, where the aircraft became almost immune from fighter intercepts and anti-aircraft fire, a drawback was that any pretence of bombing accurately went out of the window.[15] The VVS clearly gaining the ascendency by early August, bad weather between 12 and 19 of that month provided the Japanese airmen with a welcome respite.

that the fighters from either the middle or the higher group or both would find themselves in a position to dive on the Ki-27s. In turn, the Japanese reacted by putting the emphasis on formation rather than individual combat. This tactic going some way to alleviate Japanese losses and casualties, the "Boom and Zoom" tactics remained pretty much an unsolvable problem, a position summed up by Major Hidemi Yusuhara, the CO of the 24th Sentai:

If a small number of us went out, the enemy would attack. They preferred to wait until our flying time was up and we were returning, or were about to return, to base. Then they would dive from high altitude, fire blindly whether they scored hits or not, and rush home, without persisting in do-or-die tactics as we

6

ZHUKOV'S TRIUMPH

In Moscow, Stalin was determined to teach the Japanese a lesson by heavily defeating the 23rd Division and seizing the contested area. Correspondingly, reinforcements were rushed in during August. The 57th Rifle Division and the 6th Tank Brigade comprised of 245 BT-7s, 9 OT-26 flamethrower tanks, and 25 BA-10 and BA-20 armoured cars arrived in early August, and these units were followed by 1,000 men of the 212nd Airborne Brigade and the 1st Rifle Regiment. By mid-August, the, the 1st Army Group had as many as 57,000 men, 498 tanks and 385 armoured cars as well as 634 artillery pieces and mortars. There were 180 M1932 AT guns, 162 76mm regimental guns, 87 76mm M1931 and M1938 anti-aircraft guns supplemented by 64 76mm field guns, and 108 guns and howitzers with calibres ranging from 122mm to 152mm. To facilitate the transport of these weapons, the shuttle to the front was run at full speed resulting in the Soviets eventually supplying a staggering 18,000 tons of artillery shells, 6,500 tons of aircraft ammunition, 15,000 tons of lubricant, 7,500 tons of fuel and 4,000 tons of various supplies.

Among other things, this allowed the Soviet artillery to fire one round per second against enemy positions for extended periods of time, and even to increase this rate of fire to three rounds a second during shorter periods. The Soviets also built new pontoon bridges crossing the Halha River. Bringing the number of bridges to 12, it made it possible to transfer large forces from one side of the river to the other at short notice.

While weapons were brought to the front, the now Komkor Zhukov was given relatively free rein to prepare and wage the massive counter-attack that was due to take place in mid-August. It being delayed because of the adverse weather, during these preparations Zhukov noticed that the Japanese line was much stronger in the centre than on its flanks. In view of this, he opted to launch a classic double envelopment operation that would see two mobile units tasked with breaking through each enemy flank before encircling the entire enemy force. A third group was to attack the centre. Once trapped, Zhukov calculated, the 23rd Division would be destroyed.

To carry out this manoeuvre, the 1st Army Group was reorganised into four main components: two shock groups, a holding group, and a reserve. What was called the 'Northern' shock group was made up of roughly two tank battalions, an anti-tank battalion, a reinforced motor-mechanised brigade, a rifle regiment, an artillery regiment and a MPRA cavalry division. The 'Southern' shock group was even more powerful. It included a tank brigade, a motor-mechanised brigade, a rifle division, an MPRA

A Japanese officer standing at a forward observation post. (Albert Grandolini Collection)

Virtually until the end, Japanese Type 94 anti-tank guns continued to exact a heavy toll on Soviet armour. (Albert Grandolini Collection)

Table 15: 1st Army Group Order of Battle, 20 August 1939	
Units	**Notes**
1st Army Group	**CO Komkor Zhukov**
Northern Shock Group	**CO Colonel I.P. Alekseenko**
7th Motor-Mechanised Brigade	
601st Rifle Regiment	Detached from the 82nd Rifle Division
6th MPRA Cavalry Division	
82nd Artillery Regiment	Detached from the 82nd Rifle Division
Two tank battalions	Detached from 11th Tank Brigade
87th Anti-Tank Battalion	
Holding Group	CO Colonel Petrov
36th Motorised Rifle Division	24th and 149th Rifle Regiments, 175th Artillery Regiment
82nd Rifle Division	602nd and 603rd Rifle Regiments. 601st Rifle Regiment and 82nd Artillery Regiment attached to the Northern Shock Group
5th Machine Gun-Rifle Brigade	
Southern Shock Group	Colonel M.I. Potapov
57th Rifle Division	CO Colonel Galanin. 80th, 127th, 293rd Rifle Regiments, 105th Artillery Regiment, one tank battalion
8th MPRA Cavalry Division	
6th Tank Brigade	CO Colonel M.I Pavelkin. Minus the 4th Tank Battalion
8th Motor-Mechanised Brigade	
185th Artillery Regiment	
N/A SPG battalion	Equipped with SU-1-12 SPGs
37th Anti-Tank Battalion	
Rifle-Machine-Gun Battalion	Detached from the 11th Tank Brigade
One Flamethrower tank company	OT-26 tanks
Reserve	
9th Motor-Mechanised Brigade	
212th Airborne Brigade	
1st Rifle Regiment	From the 152nd Rifle Division
4th Tank battalion	Detached from the 6th Tank Brigade
Other 1st Army Group units	
85th Anti-Aircraft Regiment	
63rd Anti-Aircraft Battalion	
66th Anti-Aircraft Battalion	
150th Anti-Aircraft Battalion	
406th Communication Battalion	
937th Communication Battalion	
Separate Heavy Battery	

cavalry division, and a regiment of artillery. The holding group was composed mostly of infantry from the 36th Motorised Rifle Division and the 82nd Rifle Division, while the 1st Army Group reserve included the 9th Motor-Mechanised Brigade, the 212th Airborne Brigade, the 1st Rifle Regiment, and a tank battalion. For the full order of battle see Table 14.

Maskirovka

While Soviet units were moved away from the frontlines and underwent badly needed training to instil the basics of combined arms tactics from 1 August, a wide array of measures were introduced to confuse and mislead the Japanese regarding the forthcoming offensive. Zhukov and his closest associates kept their cards as close to their chests as they could to maintain operational secrecy, and only five officers knew the entire plan. Not until 17 August were the remainder of the most senior officers informed.

A booklet with instructions about defensive operations was widely distributed to the troops, as were related instructions broadcasted in easily breakable code. Large quantities of timber were brought into full view of the Japanese and at night, loudspeakers broadcasted noises of building work being carried out. All of this to make the Japanese believe that the 1st Army Group was preoccupied with reinforcing its defences. Every night, trucks with their silencers removed drove along the frontlines to cover other noises and to accustom the Japanese to hearing motorised movements at that time of the day. Japanese positions were harassed by heavy artillery fire each night, while the VVS buzzed overhead to stall efforts to fortify defences. The bad weather proved also immensely helpful because it impeded the Japanese from making observation flights. To keep plans as secret as possible, it was only from 18 August that the Soviet attack forces moved towards their starting positions.[1]

On the Japanese side, the Kwantung Army remained almost ignorant of the build-up taking place as it had not been provided with sufficient intelligence. Their signals intelligence did, however, intercept and decipher a message announcing a major enemy offensive in mid-August, but this failed to materialise thus sowing further confusion. A key factor was that the Japanese believed that the lack of railroads leading to the Halha River would make the kind of force concentration being put in place by the Soviets almost

Preparing for the onslaught, Japanese soldiers busily dig trench lines. Much too often, these were in exposed terrain as their commanders refused to withdraw the defensive line to more favourable ground. (Albert Grandolini Collection)

The architect of victory, Zhukov (left) posing together with Khorloogiin Choibalsan, the MPRA leader (centre). (Albert Grandolini Collection)

Soviet Riflemen preparing to move from their position under cover of a machine gun. (Albert Grandolini Collection)

impossible. Something that gave the Japanese more confidence in their ability to fight off any enemy attack was successful resistance to a series of Soviet small-scale attacks between 7 and 8 August near the confluence of the Halha and the Holsten Rivers.

The 6th Army, raised on 4 August, and placed under Lieutenant General Ogisu Rippei, became operational in mid-August. The Kwantung Army Staff also dispatched reinforcements to Hailar in the form of the 28th Infantry Regiment, a unit that already provided one of its three battalions operating under the 23rd Division command. It was followed by an artillery battalion from the 7th Division. If the Soviets were keeping their plans under cover, in early August the Kwantung Army was also seeking to implement a highly secret operation involving a detachment of Unit 731.

Known officially as the Epidemic Prevention and Water Purification Department, in reality, this group specialised in bacteriological warfare. Kwantung Army HQ sent it to Nomonhan to disseminate large quantities of the cholera bacteria around the Halha River and upstream from the Soviet bridgehead. However, there were no reports of any enemy having been affected.

The efforts of the 23rd Division to entrench itself proved anything but satisfactory. This was foremostly due to a lack of cement and timber, but the IJA's universal dislike of fighting a defensive war did not help either. To rub salt into the wound, calls from engineers to move parts of the main defensive line to less exposed areas also fell on deaf ears. Overall, a large number of positions and strongpoints were ill-suited to face the kind of firepower the RKKA was carefully massing in secrecy on the other side of the Halha River. The northern extremity of the Japanese line was covered by the 2nd and 8th Manchukuoan Cavalry Regiments, and it was anchored on the pancake shaped Fui Heights held by a mixed force of tankettes and infantry of the 23rd Reconnaissance Regiment and the 26th Infantry

Regiment. This detachment had 800 soldiers and 10 Type 38s and 41 guns. Further along the line was the 1st Battalion of the 26th Infantry Regiment which held several defensive positions between Fui and Hinomaru Heights. The heights themselves were held by the rest of the 26th Infantry Regiment, while defences were completed by the 64th and 72nd Infantry regiments based along the banks of the Holsten River. The defensive line continuing along the southern shore of the river, it was guarded by the 71st Infantry Regiment and one battalion each of the 28th Infantry Regiment and the 8th Border Garrison Unit. The southern anchor of the line was covered by the Manchukuoan 'Sekiran' Division, a mixed cavalry and infantry formation with roughly 3,000 men. Field artillery batteries and battalions were dispersed along the entire line, while heavy artillery was concentrated behind the 71st and 72nd Infantry Regiments. The only operational reserve was formed by the two remaining infantry battalions of the 28th Infantry Regiment and the bulk of the 8th Border Garrison Unit. Both were stationed in Hailar and in its surrounding areas.[2]

The "pillars of fire". Soviet artillery targets a Japanese position in preparation for an attack supported by tanks and flamethrower tanks. (Albert Grandolini Collection)

Deadly Pincers

Preparations for the Soviets' final assault started on the night of 18 August when under cover of heavy rains, the bulk of the 1st Army Group began to cross the Halha River. By dawn of 20 August, all the units ordered to carry out the offensive had arrived on the eastern shore and were spread out along a frontline stretching for some 70 kilometres. An exception was the 6th Tank Brigade whose crossing had been delayed by the selection of a pontoon that proved inadequate for tanks.

The offensive began at 0545 hours on 20 August when the weather turned hot and sunny. First, around 100 heavily escorted SB-2s bombed the Japanese front and rear positions. The Japanese responded with anti-aircraft fire allowing Soviet artillery observers to spot their positions, and once the aviation had done its work, the artillery opened with a barrage of fire from 200 guns. One of the heaviest artillery barrages witnessed since the end of the First World War, it continued unabated for more than two hours, and targeted the Japanese front and rear positions, artillery batteries as well as its anti-aircraft guns. This threw the Japanese into such confusion that their own artillery only managed to open fire an hour after

the beginning of hostilities, with many of the IJA's defences collapsing under the strain of the withering fire delivered by the Soviets. At around 0900 hours a second large air strike was launched followed by the resumption of an artillery barrage. The focus of this attack being on forward positions held by the 23rd Division, it covered the advance of Soviet infantry and armoured vehicles, as did the fog that lingered over the Halha River valley. The fog provided cover for several vehicles broadcasting the "Internationale", the "March of the Pilots" and the "March of the Artillerymen" from their loudspeakers. As to be expected, many IJA forward positions swiftly fell into Soviet hands. The first attacks were made at the centre of the IJA's defensive line by the 36th Motorised Rifle Division, the 82nd Rifle Division and the 5th Rifle-Machine Gun Brigade. The Japanese forward positions fell within a matter of hours but soon, the 26th, 64th and 72nd Infantry regiments' resistance stiffened with the help of the Japanese artillery. This was despite it being restricted to firing short barrages due to an endemic lack of ammunition, and the desire to avoid the murderous counterbattery fire. The Soviet forces did not reach their objectives on 20 August and the situation remained roughly the same over the next two days.

A situation that preoccupied Zhukov was that the Northern Shock Group had made a blunder when the group's commander, Colonel Shevnikov, ordered a three-pronged assault against Japanese positions on the Fui Heights. All started well with the Mongolian 6th Cavalry Division quickly overcoming the Manchukuoan 2nd and 8th Cavalry regiments, but when the 601st Rifle Regiment, the 11th Tank Brigade, and the 7th Motor-Mechanised Brigade attacked from the front and on the flanks, they found themselves up against the well defended positions of the 23rd Reconnaissance Regiment under Lieutenant Colonel Ioki Eiichiro. Here, around 800 Japanese troops offered extremely strong resistance, and by the evening of 20 August, the Soviets had to call off the attack. Shevnikov then made the mistake of letting himself be drawn into a pointless and bloody siege that lasted until 24 August when Eiichiro finally withdrew his forces from the Fui Heights. For Zhukov, the fault lay with Shevnikov for having underestimated the Japanese forces who had provided a "more obstinate resistance than we thought it could". Instead of "pinning the Japanese on the heights with a portion

Preparations for the onslaught: a group of BTs of the 6th Tank Brigade. (Albert Grandolini Collection)

An MPRA trooper. Both the MPRA 6th and the 8th Cavalry Divisions played a crucial role in the August victory by covering the flanks of the Soviet offensive. (Albert Grandolini Collection)

Two Japanese soldiers killed in their foxholes and photographed by the Soviets. This was a clear sign that the IJA had been badly defeated as it did everything it could to avoid the bodies of its fallen soldiers falling into enemy hands. (Albert Grandolini Collection)

of his forces and continuing to drive swiftly southwards with its main strength, the Northern Force commander kept up a series of unsuccessful assaults."[3]

The stalemate on the Northern Front forced Zhukov to draw heavily on reserves. On 23 August, the 212th Airborne Brigade was dispatched to help overcome resistance on the Fui Heights position, while the 9th Motor-Mechanised Brigade and the 4th Tank Battalion, 6th Tank Brigade were ordered to move to the area on 21 August, followed by the 11th Tank Brigade's Rifle-Machine Gun Battalion later in the day. The powerful mechanised force than flanked Fui Height and advanced toward Nomonhan did not encounter any determined resistance. Roughly six kilometres from Nomonhan, the force stumbled on a rear-depot and field hospital of the 23rd Division dispatching them quickly on 22 August, and the following day when reaching Nomonhan, it linked with the 8th Motor-Mechanised Brigade of the Southern Shock Group on 24 August, thus completing the encirclement of the 23rd Division. As for this group, it went on the attack on 20 August when the Mongolian 8th Cavalry Division made short work of the Manchukuoan Sekiran Division. Things got so bad that around 200 Manchukuoan soldiers turned against their Japanese officers, killing five before deserting. This paved the way for the 8th Motor-Mechanised Brigade to make a flanking move toward the rear of the enemy. Though the advance of the Southern Group was slowed by sandy terrain, it still managed to reach the Mongolian/Soviet-claimed border by the end of the day. It then turned south and advanced towards Nomonhan, the vicinity of which it reached the next day. In doing so, Japanese forces located south of the Holsten River found themselves entrapped. Meanwhile, the Southern Group's 57th Rifle Division had advanced head-on against positions held by the 71st Infantry Regiment. Not much progress was made on 20 August, mainly because of the late arrival of the 6th Tank Brigade and a consequential lack of armoured support.

The situation of the IJA was to worsen from 21 August as Soviet riflemen gradually managed to infiltrate its main strongholds. It was a task made easier by the fact that the 71st Infantry Regiment was badly overstretched, and this infiltration allowed the Soviets to reduce Japanese positions one after the other. Flamethrowers, tanks, and even heavy artillery were used against enemy pillboxes before survivors were finished off with grenades and small arms fire. The same methods were used to systematically dismantle the IJA's defensive line south of the Holsten River. By the end of 23 August, only one significant enemy pocket remained in the area. Worse still, by 24 August, the entire 23rd Division became surrounded as the 8th and 9th Motor-Mechanised Brigade set up in Nomonhan.[4]

An Exercise in Futility

The initial reaction of the Japanese to the Soviet offensive proved anything but decisive. On 20 August, the CO of the 23rd Division, Lieutenant General Komatsubara, identified the principles of the enemy plan and assessed the southern pincer as the most threatening. He advocated that the 72nd Infantry Regiment be removed from the centre of the defensive line so that it reinforced the 71st Infantry Regiment in the south, and he also suggested that elements of the 26th Infantry Regiment be sent to the north. This triggered a heated debate with the 6th Army commander advocating an all-out counter-attack in the south, leaving only the 64th Infantry Regiment to defend the Japanese centre and leaving the north devoid of any reinforcements. Middle ground was found on 22 August whereby a counter-attack in the south would take place at dawn on 24 August. Involving a force made up of two groups, the Right Wing was to include troops from the 23rd Division Infantry

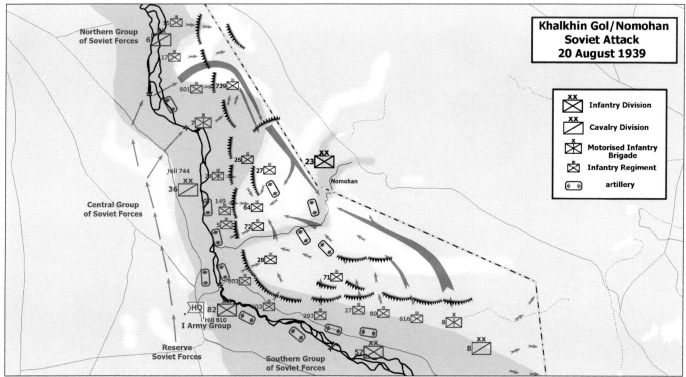

Map of the Soviet counter-attack on Khalkhin Gol/Nomonhan, on 20 August 1939. (Map by Tom Cooper)

Group HQ and from the 72nd Infantry Regiment, whereas the Left Wing would use those of the 14th Infantry Brigade HQ, and the 26th and 28th Infantry regiments, the latter arriving on foot from Hailar. These groups were to be supported by five field batteries, and four heavy artillery batteries.

The force in question was much weaker than it looked. Only the 28th Infantry Regiment was at full strength, but its members would be exhausted by their march from Hailar. The 26th and 72nd Infantry Regiments would also be exhausted. They had taken part in the drawn-out incident and the 26th Infantry Regiment only had one and a half battalions available. The remaining portion were needed on the northern shore of the Holsten to defend existing lines. Another aspect that made things difficult for the IJA was that it was short on food and ammunition. Nonetheless, 6th Army HQ remained highly confident that this would be enough to turn the table on the Soviets as illustrated by a dispatch dated 23 August sent to the Kwantung Army HQ:

Without focusing the attack on any particular point, the enemy intends to envelop us from our flanks. Its offensive effectiveness is, however, weak, and enemy artillery fire diminished after reaching a climax on afternoon of 23 August. The Sixth Army has withdrawn from the left flank in preparation for a future offensive. Our positions in other areas are being strengthened. Set your mind at ease. The Sixth Army will strike the enemy tomorrow as scheduled.

The Demise of the 72nd Infantry Regiment
The Kwantung Army Staff was obviously worried. On 23 August, the entire 7th Division was ordered to move to Hailar together with eight anti-tank companies taken from other units. The 23rd Division proceeded to place its units for the impeding counter-attack but, predictably, this proved an arduous undertaking as the Soviets attacked from all corners while their shelling constantly cut off the phone lines and disrupted communications. The lack of time meant that the Japanese could not reconnoitre enemy positions.

Their counter-offensive began mid-morning rather than dawn. Even then, not every unit, including several artillery units, had reached their assigned positions.

The infantry attacked almost unsupported in broad daylight and made its way across open terrain against unknown enemy positions. The episode gained the nickname the 'Charge of the Two Light Brigades'; around 0930 on 24 August, only the 72nd and 28th Regiment had begun their advance. Covered by fog, the 72nd Infantry Regiment made good progress, at first, and advanced around two kilometres. Once the fog lifted, however, it came under intense fire from machine guns and artillery, so much so that its components became scattered. These events were described by the logistics officer of the 23rd Division who scouted the area in the wake of the advance:

I passed many dead Japanese soldiers as I went forward, but I could not ascertain the precise location of friendly or enemy forces. When I finally reached a dune, the Soviet trenches were empty, and helmets and bodies were lying around. The entire Japanese force was already badly dispersed into small platoons, out of touch with each other and simply clinging to their gains.[5]

If things were not bad enough, the regiment was again targeted in the afternoon by the 6th Tank Brigade. The Soviets had also learned their lessons and had covered their BT-5 and BT-7 tank exhausts and ventilation fans with wire-netting. The Molotov cocktails used to great effect by the Japanese beforehand simply broke without causing damage to the engines. Another lesson that had been learned was to lock the tank hatches from the inside making it impossible for the Japanese to disable the tank by throwing grenades inside. Anti-tank weapons and field guns could be used against the tanks, but they were few in number and ammunition was in short supply. So much so that Type 92 battalion guns were used in a futile attempt to try and stop the tanks. One battery commander wrote: "Battalion guns could not destroy the tanks, and, in fact, we tried not to hit them directly. Our purpose was to convince the enemy that the Japanese

Collecting the spoils. A row of captured Type 11 LMGs. (Albert Grandolini Collection)

Two out of the several dozen guns either destroyed or captured by the Soviets after their formations fell on Japanese batteries. (Albert Grandolini Collection)

were still in business. It was a kind of camouflage effort to conceal our actual weakness in firepower."[6]

By the end of the afternoon, the state of confusion had become so bad that the even the regimental headquarters was threatened. Its CO, Colonel Sakai, had to order the burying of the colours to avoid the risk of seeing them captured and, finally, the unit was ordered to withdraw. It was a spent force. Of the 1,295 men taking part on 24

August, 323 were killed and another 377 wounded representing a casualty rate of more than 50 percent.

As for the Right Wing, the 28th Infantry Regiment initially made good progress and took the enemy first line of defence by using infiltration tactics, before being stopped cold by heavy rifle and machine gun fire from the 80th Rifle Regiment and constant shelling. The arrival in the afternoon of the 26th Infantry Regiment did not

Another of the Japanese "heavies" captured and inspected by Soviet officers. (Albert Grandolini Collection)

lead to further progress being made. The Japanese counter-attack of 24 August dismally failed, therefore, while the Soviets were just about to complete their double envelopment manoeuvre. Incredibly enough, a similar offensive – involving only the 14th Brigade – was organised for the next day. The reason for this was that Lieutenant General Komatsubara saw it as the as the only way to counter the increasing threat to his troops. The 26th and 28th Regiments launched a second assault on 25 August. This time, they managed to capture a series of Soviet positions thanks, in part, to much better artillery support than the previous day. Nevertheless, the attack ended in the face of superior enemy firepower and counterattacks by the 6th Tank Brigade. Meanwhile, the 1st Regiment was sent to reinforce the 80th Rifle Regiment. As for the 14th Brigade, it remained in position for the next few days where, until 29 August, it tried desperately to fend off armour-supported Soviet counterattacks. Defeated, it pulled back to positions it occupied from 24 August. It had lost half of its manpower for no gain.[7]

The VVS's day of Triumph

20 August also saw the massive involvement of the VVS. At first, a formation of nine SB-2s deliberately overflew the battlefield to attract Japanese anti-aircraft fire, until a group of 36 I-16s attacked the unmasked anti-aircraft batteries. The flyovers paved the way for 150 SB-2 bombers escorted by a similar number of fighters from the 22nd, 56th and 70th IAP. They attacked the 23rd Division's front- and rear-guard positions before making way for Soviet artillery. A second wave of 52 SB-3s and 167 fighters was launched at 0845 and, once more, they targeted Japanese entrenchments. Thereafter, groups of between 18 and 27 SB-2s, all heavily escorted, continued to appear over the battlefield during the day. As for the fighters, their mission was to make strafing runs. At approximately 1600 a group of 20 I-16s attacked Hosiu Airfield, the base of the 64th Sentai destroying or damaging at least five Ki-27s. The IJAAC did not remain passive, however, and it scrambled all the fighters it could muster to counter the Soviet aerial juggernaut. With limited results, as the VVS lost only five fighters to all causes, while three SB-2s were damaged. The Japanese fighter pilots were overwhelmed and were limited to escorting their small bomber formations or devising tactics to limit their own casualties. The events were recalled by Lieutenant Colonel Matsumura Kojiro, a former CO of the 24th Sentai:

At the time of the large-scale Russian attacks, we committed every plane we had. While we were out in force, flying our four daily one-hour sorties, the enemy did not challenge us. Instead, they resorted to using effective guerrilla tactics – catching bombers alone, always seeking weak points, employing small forces, and avoiding pitched battles. We did not counter-attack; it was not worth it since we were conserving our aircraft. Thus, friendly ground forces may have felt that the Russians controlled the air, but that was not really true.[8]

Still, the 2nd Hiko Shidan managed to launch four air raids to support the ground troops that day. Six Ki-30s of the 10th Sentai bombed a Soviet forward airfield on the western shore of the Halha River, and 11 Ki-21s of the 61st Sentai attacked Soviet troops near the confluence between the two rivers. Another two small formations of Ki-30s from the 10th and 16th Sentai attacked Soviet forces during the day.

The formations remaining unscathed thanks to their fighter escorts but their attacks were a mere trickle compared to the amount of firepower the VVS was using on the battlefield, and from the events of 20 August it became obvious that the Soviets had gained air supremacy. In all, the VVS flew 1,094 sorties on that day including 350 made by bombers and 744 by fighters.

The Failed Operation S

Once authorised on 7 August to strike targets in uncontested Mongolian territory, the 2nd Hiko Shidan began to prepare a new wave of attacks against VVS airfields, codenamed Operation S. However, the exhaustion of the division's units was such that the raid could not be undertaken before the Soviet Offensive of 20 August. Finally, it took place at dawn on 21 August when 36 Ki-30s and Ki-21s escorted by Ki-27s headed towards the Tamsag Bulak airfields. The Soviets were not taken by surprise, and by the time the Japanese arrived they had 200 fighters in the air. The Japanese fighters managed to keep the Soviet pilots away from their bombers, but the latter failed to inflict any significant damage to the airfields. A much smaller follow-up raid occurred at approximately 1100 and triggered a new series of dogfights between Japanese and Soviet fighters. In the afternoon, both sides reverted their efforts to supporting their respective ground forces. The 2nd Hiko Shidan did dispatch another group of bombers against Tamsag Bulak on 22 August but their bombs fell on empty airfields. In terms of losses, despite their own wildly optimistic claims of having destroyed 109 Soviet aircraft, the raids launched by the Japanese failed miserably. Indeed, the Soviets lost only seven fighters and five bombers with one of each being destroyed on 22 August. This was a relatively small number of aircraft to lose considering the VVS flew 1,138 sorties on 21 August alone. As for Japanese losses, they amounted to 14 over a two-day period. This was unsustainable considering their numerical inferiority, Japanese pilots were so exhausted that several officers requested a ceasefire to rest crews and to tend overworked machines. Predictably, given the increasingly disastrous situation unfolding on the battlefield this was overruled. Accordingly, both Japanese bombers and fighters continued to throw all they could at Nomonhan. On 23 August, 68 Ki-30 and 17 Ki-30 sorties took place and pilots flew as many as five missions per day. A pace that continued until the end of the land battle, between 23 August and 1 September the four bomber Sentais managed to drop a total of 706 15kg bombs, 4,362 50kg and 75 100kg bombs but at an unsustainable price: 43 aircraft were lost between 20 and 31 August, and 29 pilots were either killed or grievously wounded.

The frontlines stabilising after the demise of the 23rd Division, large-scale air combats continued unabated until the truce of 16 September. The rate of flights was slower compared to the August peaks. Ironically, it was also during this period that the 2nd Hiko Shidan was reinforced. On 26 August, the 33rd Sentai with 31 obsolete Ki-10 fighters was ordered to the Nomonhan area where it arrived on 30 August. It was followed by the 9th Sentai (30 Ki-10s), the 29th Sentai (six Ki-15s), the 65th Sentai (16 Ki-32s), the 45th Sentai (28 Ki-32s), and the 59th Sentai (Ki-27s). This influx of new units enticed the Kwantung Army to order a new 'aerial extermination action', this time to strengthen the Japanese hand on the negotiating table.

If, on 14 September, some 30 Ki-30s escorted by 45 fighters attacked Soviet forward airfields, no damage was caused and there were no casualties on either side. That changed the following day, on the other hand, when the 2nd Hiko Shidan intensified its efforts. Around 0920, a heavily escorted formation of Ki-30s and Ki-32s attacked airfields in the Tamsag Bulak area surprising Soviet forces that failed to intercept them. A second attack saw Ki-21s from the 61st Sentai escorted by Ki-27s of the 11th and 64th Sentai. They shot down three I-153s of the 56th IAP just after their take-off.

Several other dogfights took place during the day, and the VVS emerged as a clear-cut victor. This was primarily because the 59th Sentai's second chutai was attacked by several dozen I-16s as it flew at low altitude. The Soviets managed to shoot down six Ki-27s in short order, killing five pilots. By the end of the day, the VVS had lost six fighters, five of them I-153s, while the IJAAC lost nine fighters and one bomber. With this, the nine-month Nomonhan air battle was over.

The battle finished in an overall draw in terms of casualties, but it was clear that the Soviets had gained overall air supremacy. The VVS flew a total of 20,524 combat missions between 21 May and 15 September 1939, and significantly, 14,458 of those took place between 20 August and 15 September. During their 2,015 combat missions, the Soviet bombers dropped a total of 1,298 tons of bombs at a cost of 52 SB-2s and one TB-3 that were lost in combat or accidents. As for fighters, 109 I-16s, 65 I-15bis, 22 I-153s and one R-5 were also lost. The Japanese flew about half that number of missions and lost 164 aircraft with 152 airmen killed or missing in action. The six fighter Sentais which took part in the incident lost 63 pilots but claimed a staggering 1,093 certain and 209 probable victories.[9]

Rings of Steel

While the 14th Brigade was exhausting itself by carrying out doomed counterattacks, the 1st Army Group forces had continued their advance and had succeeded in splitting the 23rd Division into three main pockets. The Soviets first focused on attacking Japanese positions south of the Holsten River, and by the evening of 27 August, they had largely managed to do so, and Japanese units were retreating to the northern side of the river. That day, the Japanese lost all hopes of reversing the flow of the battle after having thrown their last available reserves into the fire. The 7th Division's remaining units – the 13th Brigade with the 25th and 27th Infantry regiments and the 7th Field Artillery Regiment – with approximately 5,000 men, had moved from Hailar to Chiangchunmiao before launching an attack against the outer southern section of the ring enclosing the 23rd Division. However, the attack was repulsed by the MPRA's 6th Cavalry Division, the 601st Rifle Regiment, and the 11th Tank Brigade after a day of intense fighting. To follow up, on 27 August, Zhukov ordered forces to concentrate their fire on the remaining Japanese forces on the northern side of the Holsten. The 24th, 127th, 149th and 601st Rifle Regiments, plus the 5th Rifle-Machine Gun Brigade and the 9th Motor-Mechanised Brigade then converged on the remaining Japanese pockets and gradually overwhelmed the fierce resistance of the beleaguered enemy. This was done by resuming the standard tactics of methodically isolating Japanese strongpoints before pounding them with concentrated artillery fire and sending in tanks and infantry. On 28 August, the highly symbolic Remizov Heights fell. Their loss led to Colonel Yamagata ordering the regimental colours to be buried and his suicide. The next day, Lieutenant Colonel Higashi Munehar of the 71st Infantry Regiment led a suicide charge after also having buried his regiment's colours. Another commander who attempted to repeat this gesture was Lieutenant General Komatsubara of the 23rd Division. Nevertheless, he was forbidden from doing so and, instead, managed to escape the battlefield on 30-31 August along with 400 of his men.

On 31 August, Zhukov was able to announce that the contested area had been cleared of Japanese troops, and the 1st Army Group began to entrench itself along the Mongolian/Soviet-claimed border. The 23rd Division was finished as a cohesive fighting unit and the IJA had suffered its worst defeat ever.[10] Only on 26 August did Kwantung Army HQ learn of the true strength of the 1st Army Group, thanks to documents captured on a dead Soviet officer. Not deterring it in the least, reinforcements were sent to the 6th Army on a massive level from more important parts of Manchuria. The entire 2nd and 4th Divisions were ordered to Hailar along with an infantry regiment and an artillery battalion from the 1st Division which formed the Goto Detachment, as well as all the available heavy artillery regiments. Acting in unison with the 7th Division and the remnants of the 23rd Division, these forces formed a defensive line situated along the Soviet-claimed border. Both the 6th Army and the Kwantung Army HQ were hell-bound into launching an all-out counter-attack to expel the Soviets from the eastern bank of the Halha River. This was scheduled for the 10 September and was planned to include a series of attacks over several nights. The intent of Lieutenant General Ogisu was made crystal clear in a communiqué given to the troops on 5 September:

The Commanding General of the Kwantung Army decided this autumn to help us by sending well-trained troops stationed in

Manchuria. He has transferred them to where the future battle will take place and has placed them under my command. The Army has only one way of carrying out its actions, and that is to make the army unanimous and consolidated to deliver a crushing blow to eliminate the enemy's growing insolence. The Army will greet the coming autumn by finishing off this mouse with one blow and will proudly show the world the might of the imperial troops.[11]

Despite this belligerence, cooler heads were to prevail, and for the AGS, enough was enough even though Tokyo transferred the 5th and 14th divisions from China and Japan respectively and approved the Kwantung Army's decision to dispatch new divisions to the contested area.

The fall of the first snows on 9 September, and the obvious inability to sustain such a large force in the area not only made the whole counter-attack plan illusory, but it risked an all-out war against the Soviet Union just after the signing of the Soviet-German Pact of non-aggression. Attacking the Soviet Union would have been outright suicidal, so an Imperial Order was issued explicitly forbidding any aggressive action. The number of Japanese troops stationed near the border was to be kept to a minimum, and for good measure the entire Kwantung Army high command was replaced in days starting with its commander and its Chief of Staff who were ordered back to Tokyo.

Concurrently, the Japanese Ambassador in Moscow was instructed to begin negotiations to bring about a swift ending to the incident. Negotiations began on 9 September and proved especially efficient as Stalin did not have any intention of prolonging the conflict. By 15 September, both sides had agreed to a ceasefire based upon the positions held by each belligerent at the time. Also, a joint commission was handed the mission of establishing the border. At 0200 on 16 September hostilities ceased altogether and both sides began an exchange of prisoners and those killed. The incident concluded the worst defeat ever suffered by the Imperial Japanese Army at that time.[12]

While paling in comparison to the bloodshed of the coming years, the Nomonhan Incident proved costly for both the Soviets and the Japanese. According to the 6th Army's Medical Bureau the Japanese suffered approximately 20,000 casualties – 7,696 killed, 8,647 wounded, 2,350 died of sickness, and 1,021 missing in action. The 23rd Division bore the brunt of these casualties and 4,976 out of its 15,975 men were killed during the incident. This was staggering considering that 75,378 men took part in the conflict. Whereas combat units were affected the most, only 300 men of the 26th Infantry Regiment were left out of roughly 1,500 at the end of August.

Almost all the 23rd Division's weaponry and most of its heavy artillery were also lost, but perhaps the biggest casualty was that the entire IJA doctrine had collapsed with the defeat of the 23rd Division. This said, the Army failed to draw the necessary conclusions and it was only by sheer luck that it proved to be well-suited to the initial stages of the Pacific War. Perhaps even more surprising is that the victors suffered as much as the vanquished. This was partly because of the fanatical resistance offered by the Japanese troops. In effect, 9,703 Soviet soldiers were either killed, or went missing in action during the incident. Another 15,952 were wounded while the MPRA lost 165 men and a further 391 were wounded. Losses of equipment of various kinds were extensive too: 14 artillery pieces were destroyed and, importantly, a staggering 236 BT-5s, BT-7s and T-26 tanks were destroyed or in need of extensive repairs, as were 150 armoured cars and tankettes. Despite all the lessons drawn from the battle in early July, the losses in August remained heavy with the 11th Tank Brigade alone seeing 114 BT-5s and BT-7s either destroyed or damaged between 20 and 30 August 1939, mostly due to enemy anti-tank and field artillery fire. The relative parity in losses could not hide the fact that Moscow won a strategic victory of staggering proportions as it greatly contributed to securing the Soviet Union's eastern borders from any new Japanese infringement for years to come.[13]

BIBLIOGRAPHY

Albaret, L., "Ces Français qui façonnèrent l'aviation militaire japonaise", in *Le Fana de l'aviation*, n° 600, November 2019

Baeza, B., *Les avions de l'armée impériale japonaise* (Outreau, Lela Presse, 2011)

Bernard, N., *La guerre germano-soviétique 1941-1945* (Paris, Éditions Tallandier, 2013)

Bernard, N., *La guerre du Pacifique 1941-1945* (Paris, Éditions Tallandier, 2016)

Birolli, B., *Ishiwara: L'homme qui déclencha la guerre* (Birolli, 2019)

Bond, B., Tachikawa, K., *British and Japanese Military Leadership in the Far Eastern War 1941-1945* (Abingdon, Frank Cass, 2004)

Coox, A., D., *Nomonhan; Japan against Russia, 1939* (Stanford, Stanford University Press, 1985)

Colvin, J., *Nomonhan* (London, Quarted Books, 1999)

Department of the Army, National Ground Intelligence Center, Classification of secrecy has been removed: losses suffered by USSR Armed Forces in wars, combat operations, and military conflicts (Charlottesville, 1996)

Drea, E., *Japan's Imperial Army: Its Rise and Fall, 1853-1945* (Lawrence, University Press of Kansas, 2009)

Drea E., *Nomonhan: Japanese-Soviet Tactical Combat, 1939* (Fort Leavenworth, US Army Command and General Staff College, 1981)

Drea, E., *In the Service of the Emperor: Essays on the Imperial Japanese Army* (Lincoln, University of Nebraska Press, 2003)

Erickson, J., *The Soviet High-Command; A Military-Political History 1918-1941* (Oxon, Frank Cass Publishers, 2001)

Fontanellaz, A. "Chugata Sensha; Chars moyens de l'Armée impériale japonaise", *Batailles et Blindés*, no 73, June-July 2016

Fontanellaz, A., *Red Star versus Rising Sun, Volume 1: The Conquest of Manchuria 1931-1938* (Warwick: Helion & Company Publishing, 2021)

Glantz, D., *The Soviet Airborne Experience* (Fort Leavenworth, Combat Studies Institute, 1984)

Glantz, D., *The Motor-Mechanization program of the Red Army during the interwar years* (Fort Leavenworth, Soviet Army Studies Office, 1990)

Goldman, S., *Nomonhan 1939: the Red Army's victory that shaped Second World War* (Annapolis, Naval Institute Press, 2012)

Gustavsson, H., *Sino-Japanese Air War; 1937-1945 The Longest Struggle* (Fonthill Media Limited, 2016)

Harries M. & S., *Soldiers of the Sun: The Rise and fall of the Imperial Japanese Army* (New York, Random House, 1992)

Hata, I., Izawa, Y., Shores, C., *Japanese Army Air Force Fighter Units and their Aces 1931-1945* (London, Grub Street, 2002)

Higham, R., Harris S. J, *Why Air Forces Fail: The Anatomy of Defeat* (Lexington, The University Press of Kentucky, 2006)

Hill, A., *The Red Army and the Second World War* (Cambridge: Cambridge University Press, 2019)

Hooton, E.R., *Stalin's claws: From the purges to the Winter War: Red Army operations before Barbarossa 1937-1941* (Pulborough, Tattered Flag Press, 2013)

Jowett P., *Rays of the Rising Sun; Armed forces of Japan's Asian Allies 1931-45, Vol.1 China and Manchukuo* (Solihull, Helion & Company Ltd, 2004)

Kolomiets, M., "Boi u reki Khalkin-Gol", Frontovaya Illyustratsiya/Frontline Illustration, 2/2002

Kotani, K., "Japanese intelligence and the Soviet-Japanese border conflicts in the 1930s", *NIDS Military History Studies Annual*, no 11, March 2008

Kotelnikov,V., *Air War Over Khalkhin Gol: The Nomonhan Incident* (Bedford, SAM Publications, 2010)

Kotelnikov, V., "Etoiles rouges contre Soleil levant", *Batailles Aériennes*, no 50, October-November-December 2009.

Lee, C., "Counterinsurgency in Manchuria: the Japanese experience, 1931-1940", Memorandum RM-5012-ARPA, January 1967

Lopez J., Otkhmezuri L., *Joukov; l'homme qui a vaincu Hitler* (Perrin, 2013)

Lopez J., Otkhmezuri L., *Les Maréchaux de Staline* (Paris, Perrin, 2021)

Margolin, J-L., *L'armée de l'Empereur: Violences et crimes du Japon en guerre 1937-1945* (Paris, Armand Colin, 2007)

Maslov, M., *Polikarpov I-15, I-16 and I-153 Aces* (Oxford, Osprey Publishing, 2010)

McDonald, A., *Where the War was won: Nomonhan 1939* (London, Austin Macauley Publishers Ltd, 2017)

Mellinger, G.M., "Soviet Air Order of Battle for the Khalkin Gol Incident" in J-aircraft.com, consulted 10 August 2021

Millman, N., *Ki-27 "Nate" Aces* (Oxford, Osprey Publishing, 2013)

Nedialkov, D., *In the Skies of Nomonhan; Japan versus Russia May-September 1939* (Manchester, Crecy Publishing Limited, 2011)

Ness, L., Rikugun, *Guide to Japanese Ground Forces 1937-1945; Volume 1: Tactical Organization of Imperial Japanese Army & Navy Ground Forces* (Solihull, Helion & Company Limited, 2014)

Office of the Chief of Military History, Department of the Army, Japanese Studies on Manchuria, Vol. XI, Part 3, Book A; Small Wars and Border Problems; the Changkufeng Incident, 9 July 1956

Office of the Chief of Military History, Department of the Army, Japanese Studies on Manchuria, Vol. XI, Part 3, Book B; Small Wars and Border Problems; The Nomonhan Incident

Office of the Chief of Military History, Department of the Army, Japanese Studies on Manchuria, Vol. XI, Part 3, Book C; Small Wars and Border Problems; The Nomonhan Incident

Office of the Chief of Military History, Department of the Army, Japanese Special Studies on Manchuria, Vol. XIII, Study of Strategical and tactical peculiarities on Far Eastern Russia and Soviet Far East Forces, January 1955

Paine, S.C.M., *The Wars for Asia 1911-1949* (Cambridge, Cambridge University Press, 2012)

Peattie, M., R., *Sunburst: The Rise of Japanese Naval Air Power, 1909-1941* (Annapolis: Naval Institute Press, 2007) Kotelnikov (2009)

Polak C., "La mission militaire française de l'aéronautique au Japon (1919-1921)", *Ebitsu*, No 51/2014, online version 1 November 2014

Prenatt J., *Soviet Armoured Cars 1936-45* (Oxford, Osprey Publishing, 2020)

Rottman, G., Takizawa, A., *Second World War Japanese Tank Tactics* (Oxford, Osprey Publishing, 2008)

Sapir, J., *La Mandchourie oubliée; grandeur et démesure de l'art de la guerre soviétique* (Monaco, éditions du Rocher, 1996)

Schultz, R., "Because We Were Japanese Soldiers": The Failure of Japanese Tactics at Changkufeng and Nomonhan and Lessons Left Unlearned (Honours Thesis, Oberlin College Department of History, 2011)

Sterret, J., "Soviet Air Force Operational Theory; 1918-1945" (Kings College, Department of War Studies, London, 2004)

Worden R., Savada A., *Mongolia: a country study* (Washington, Library of Congress, 1991)

Zaloga, S., J., *Japanese Tanks 1939-45* (Oxford, Osprey Publishing, 2007)

NOTES

Addendum/Errata to volume 1

1 Lopez and Otkhmezuri (2021), p.123.

2 Lopez and Otkhmezuri (2021), p.125.

3 Lopez and Otkhmezuri, (2021), pp.122–125.

4 Nedialkov, pp.10–11.

Introduction

1 Office of the Chief of Military History, Department of the Army, Japanese Special Studies on Manchuria, Vol. XIII, Study of Strategical and tactical peculiarities on Far Eastern Russia and Soviet Far East Forces, January 1955, *p.45*.

Chapter 1

1 The other sections were the 2nd Section (Intelligence), the 3rd Section (Logistics) and the 4th Section (Manchukuoan affairs), respectively led by Lieutenant Colonel Isomura Takesuke, Colonel Isoya Goro and Lieutenant Colonel Katakura Tadashi. Office of the Chief of Military History, Department of the Army, Japanese Studies on Manchuria, Vol. XI, Part 3, Book B, "Small Wars and Border Problems; The Nomonhan Incident". pp.170–175.

2 Coox (1985), pp.1112–1116.

3 Goldman (2012), p.85.

4 *Japanese Studies on Manchuria, Book B*, pp.195–196.

5 In triangular divisions, the single Brigade HQ was intended to ease the splitting of the division into two different forces if needed.

6 Coox (1985), pp.174–181, 1104–1116; Goldman (2012), pp.83–87; Japanese Studies on Manchuria, Vol. XI, Part 3, Book B, pp.170–175, 180–183, 190–203; Ness (2014), pp.17, 22, 67; Ness (2015), pp.132, 137, McDonald (2017), p.211.

7 *Japanese Special Studies in Manchuria, Volume XIII*, pp.56–57, and J. Erickson (2001), p.517.

8 Hill, p.105.

9 See volume 1 of this mini-series for further background on the development of the 57th KON and MPRA.

Chapter 2

1 Japanese Studies on Manchuria vol. XI, Part 3, Book C, pp.567, 570–571; Japanese Studies on Manchuria vol. XI, Part 3, Book B, pp.204–210, 213; Goldman (2012), pp.80–83, 92; Coox (1985), pp.143–145.

2 Coox (1985), pp.149–157; V. Kotelnikov (2010), pp.4–6.

3 Coox (1985), pp.189–194, 197–198; Goldman (2012), pp.88–90; Japanese Studies on Manchuria vol. XI, Part 3, Book B, pp.215–217, 219–220.

4 *Japanese Studies on Manchuria, vol. XI, Part 3, Book B*, pp.233–239; Book C, pp.573–574; Hooton (2013), p.50; Goldman (2012), pp.94–95.

5 *Japanese Studies on Manchuria vol. XI, Part 3, Book B*, p.235.

6 Japanese Studies on Manchuria vol. XI, Part 3, Book B, pp.221–222, 226; Book C, pp.573–576; Goldman (2012), pp.93–96; Coox (1985), pp.203–206; Hooton (2013), p.50; Lopez & Otkhmezuri (2013), p.222; Prenatt (2020), p.38.

7 Japanese Studies on Manchuria vol. XI, Part 3, Book B, p.228; Book C, p.577; Goldman (2012), pp.97–98 Coox (1985), pp.206–211.

8 These losses are those mentioned in Kolomiets, M., "Boi u reki Khalkin-Gol", Frontovaya Illyustratsiya/Frontline Illustration, 2/2002 via AMVAS, http://www.armchairgeneral.com/rkkaww2/, accessed 1 July 2021. There are huge discrepancies in the reported losses for both sides in the various engagements.

9 Lopez & Otkhmezuri (2013), pp.222–223, (author's translation).

10 Japanese Studies on Manchuria vol. XI, Part 3, Book B, pp.229, 231, 236; Book C, pp.577–578; Goldman (2012), pp.98, 99,100–103; Coox (2015), pp.237, 238, 239, 242; Hooton (2013), p.51; Erickson (2001), pp.518–519; Lopez & Otkhmezuri (2013), pp.217–224.

Chapter 3

1 Lopez & Otkhmezuri (2013), pp.230–231, 234; Goldman (2012), pp.49, 54, 156–159; Hooton (2013), p.52; Japanese Studies on Manchuria vol. XI, Part 3, Book C pp.578–580; Erickson (2001), pp.519–520; Kolomiets.

2 *Japanese Studies on Manchuria vol. XI, Part 3, Book B* pp.267–268.

3 *Japanese Studies on Manchuria vol. XI, Part 3, Book* B, pp.247–250, 259, 266–268; Goldman (2012), pp.102–103, 107, 110–111; Coox (1985), pp.254, 256, 258, 266, 268–273, 279–282; McDonald (2017), pp.203–204.

4 Coox (1985), pp.279–280.

5 Goldman (2012), p.110.

6 Goldman (2012), p.111.

7 Coox (1985), pp.18, 290, 310, 349–350; Goldman (2012), pp.105, 112; McDonald (2017), pp.205–206, 210–211; Japanese Studies on Manchuria vol. XI, Part 3, Book B, pp.260–263; Rottman & Takizawa pp.5, 7–8.

8 Coox (1985), pp.285, 287, 290; Goldman (2012), pp.104, 112, 115; Hooton (2013), pp.48, 53–54; McDonald (2017), pp.205, 210–212, 226.

9 Japanese Studies on Manchuria vol. XI, Part 3, Book B, pp.289–293; McDonald (2017) pp.213–214; Coox (1985), pp.289, 291, 293, 296–297, 299.

10 Coox (1985), p.384.

11 Coox (1985), p.384, 380.

12 Japanese Studies on Manchuria vol. XI, Part 3, Book B, pp.303–305; Japanese Studies on Manchuria vol. XI, Part 3, Book C, p.583; Coox (1985) pp.363, 366–369, 372, 376, 379, 381, 384, 386, 388, 391, 394.

13 Erickson (2001), p.520; Japanese Studies on Manchuria vol. XI, Part 3, Book C pp.580–585; Lopez & Otkhmezuri (2013), pp.239, 241.

14 Lopez and Otkhmezuri (2013), pp.241, (author's translation).

15 Coox (1985), p.306.

16 Japanese Studies on Manchuria vol. XI, Part 3, Book B, pp.293–294, 297–298; Book C, pp.585–586; Coox (1985), pp.299–301, 305, 311, 316; Erickson (2001), p.521; Goldman (2012), p.116; Hill, pp.95–97; Hooton (2013), pp.54–55.

17 Japanese Studies on Manchuria vol. XI, Part 3, Book B, pp.297, 299, 300, 303; Goldman (2012), pp.119–120; Coox (1985), pp.332. 335, 342; Hooton (2013), p.55; Soviet losses are those reported in Kolomiets via AMVAS.

18 *Japanese Studies on Manchuria vol. XI, Part 3, Book B*, pp.306–311.

19 Kolomiets, Japanese Studies on Manchuria vol. XI, Part 3, Book B, p.304; Hooton (2013), p.56; Goldman (2012), pp.117–119; McDonald (2017), pp.239–241; Coox (1985), pp.398–400, 404–406, 409.

20 Japanese Studies on Manchuria vol. XI, Part 3, Book B, p.305; Japanese Studies on Manchuria vol. XI, Part 3, Book C, pp.588–589; Goldman (2012), pp.125–126; Hooton (2013), p.56; McDonald (2017), pp.243–243, 247–250, 252; Coox (1985), pp.468, 474, 476, 477; Kolomiets.

21 Japanese Studies on Manchuria vol. XI, Part 3, Book B, pp.319, 320–323; Japanese Studies on Manchuria vol. XI, Part 3, Book C, p.590; Coox (1985), pp.491–493, 502–503, 525, 545; Goldman (2012), pp.126–127, 129; Hooton (2013), p.57; McDonald (2017), pp.254, 255, 257 259; Ness (2014), pp.287, 293; (Ness (2015), pp.141–142, 144; Kolomiets.

22 Japanese Studies on Manchuria vol. XI, Part 3, Book B, p.319; Japanese Studies on Manchuria vol. XI, Part 3, Book C, pp.590–591; Coox (1985), pp.503, 506, 511, 514, 517, 520, 547; Erickson (2001), p.521; Goldman (2012), pp.127–128; Hooton (2013), p.57; McDonald (2017), pp.254, 256–260; Kolomiets.

23 *Japanese Studies on Manchuria vol. XI, Part 3, Book B, pp.336–337.*

24 Coox (1985), p.25.

25 Japanese Studies on Manchuria vol. XI, Part 3, Book B, pp.334–337, 348; Coox (1985), p.25; Goldman (2012), pp.129–131; McDonald (2017), pp.261–262.

Chapter 4

1 Albaret (2019); Baeza (2011), pp.9–10, 18, 20, 23, 27–30; Bond & Tachikawa (2004), p.132; Hata, Izawa and Shores (2002), pp.1, 102; Higham & Harris (2006), pp.180–182; Polak.

2 Baeza (2011), pp.10–11, 14; Bond & Tachikawa (2004), p.132; Drea (2009) p.154, Hata, Izawa and Shores (2002), pp.1–2, 4; Higham & Harris (2006), p.182; Polak.

3 Table adapted from Baeza (2011), p.14.

4 Bond & Tachikawa (2004), pp.132–134; Higham & Harris (2006), pp.179, and pp.182–186.

5 Baeza (2011) p.15; Hata, Izawa and Shores (2002), pp.X, XI, 5–6, 10; Gustavsson (2016), pp.62, 65–66; Japanese Monograph no 76, pp.3–12, 18–23, 36–37.

6 The 9th and 10th for the fighters and the 16th, 17th and 18th for the reconnaissance aircraft.

7 Table adapted from Baeza (2011), pp.511–518.

8 Baeza (2011) pp.18, 57, 129, 138–146; Paettie, pp.23–24.

9 Millman (2013), p.12.

10 Millman (2013), p.23 Sen is the abbreviation for the Japanese word "Sentoki", which means "fighter".

11 This subchapter is drawn from Baeza (2011), pp.104–106, 125–131, 138–146, 147–157, 188–193; otherwise Hata, Izawa and Shores (2002), p.10; Millman pp.7–9, 12, 23; Nedialkov, pp.20, 23–26.

12 Japanese Studies on Manchuria vol. XI, Part 3, Book B, p.178; Baeza (2011) p.14; Hata, Izawa and Shores (2002), pp.2, 4, 13, Coox (1985), pp.84, 194, 684; Nedialkov, p.11.

13 M. Maslov (2010), p.28.

14 Erickson (2001), pp.75, 151, 161, 175–176, 340, 382, 408–409; Hill, pp.34–35, 38–39; Hooton (2013), pp. IX, 7, 11; Nedialkov, pp.16–18; Sterrett, pp.21–25, 29, 39, 74–75.

15 J. Sterrett, "Soviet Air Force Operational Theory; 1918–1945" p.36.

16 Erickson (2001), pp.382–383, 437, 439–440; Hooton (2013), pp.1, 28; Maslov (2010), pp.33, 40; Sterrett, pp.41, 51, 72, 108, 114–115, 119–122.

17 Maslov (2010), pp.10–12.

18 Nedialkov, p.22.

19 Maslov (2010), pp.7–12, 16, 18, 24–26, 30–33; Nedialkov; pp.21–22, 26–27, 32, 152–156, 159; Kotelnikov (2009), p.79.

20 Nedialkov, pp.28–31, 179, 182, 184–186, 188, 190–191; Kotelnikov (2009), p.80.

21 Nedialkov, "pp.16–18, and V. Kotelnikov (2010), pp.8–10

Chapter 5

1 The Soviets did mention the incident although it may have been a Mongolian aircraft. This was the first of countless occasions when Japanese and Soviet records differed markedly, with sometimes one side reporting large-scale engagements while the other side did not acknowledge any aerial activity. This, as well as the propensity of both sides to take overclaims at face value makes any detailed, blow by blow narration of the air war a challenging undertaking to say the least.

2 Maslov (2010), p.43.

3 Japanese Studies on Manchuria vol. XI, Part 3, Book B, pp.219, 224; Coox (1985), pp.202, 203; Nedialkov, pp.34, 36, 38–43; Kotelnikov (2009), pp.15, 18, 20–21; Hata, Izawa & Shores (2002), pp.14–15; Millman (2013), pp.17–20, 22; Maslov (2010), pp.42–43.

4 Maslov (2010), p.44; Nediakov, pp.43, 44, 46, 48, 49, 50, 54–55; Kotelnikov (2009), pp.23–24, Melinger.

5 Millman (2013), p.24.

6 Maslov (2010), pp.44–45.

7 Japanese Studies on Manchuria vol. XI, Part 3, Book B, pp.262, 264; Coox (1985), pp.256, 266, 271–273; Nedialkov, pp.46, 50–57; Kotelnikov (2009); pp.24–27; Hata, Izawa & Shores (2002), pp.15–26, 283, Millman (2013), p.25; Maslov (2010), pp.44–45.

8 Japanese Studies on Manchuria vol. XI, Part 3, Book B, pp.264–266, 271–274, Coox (1985), pp.256, 273–276; Nedialkov pp.59, 62, Kotelnikov (2009) p.33; Hata, Izawa, and Shores (2002), p.283; Millman, pp.26, 28.

9 Hata, Izawa and Shores (2002), pp.17, 283; Millman (2010), p.29; Kotelnikov (2009), pp.39–43; Nedialkov pp.66–72

10 Hata, Izawa and Shores (2002), pp.17–18, 283; Millman (2010), p.30, 31; Kotelnikov (2009), pp.46, 48, 50, 51, 52; Nedialkov; pp.73,74, 83, 85, 89, 88, 90. Three Ki-15s were also destroyed during a surprise VVS strafing attack against their airfield on 23 July.

11 Japanese Studies on Manchuria vol. XI, Part 3, Book B, p.345; Hata, Izawa and Shores (2002), p.18; Hill, pp.116–117; Kotelnikov (2009), pp.39–40, 46, 49–50, 54, Nedialkov, pp.73, 79–82, 93.

12 Adapted from Mellinger, "Soviet Air Order of Battle for the Khalkin Gol Incident".

13 Japanese Studies on Manchuria vol. XI, Part 3, Book B, p.339; Hata, Izawa and Shores (2002), pp.18, 284, Millman (2010), pp.31, 38; Kotelnikov (2009), p.54; Nedialkov, pp.90–91, 95–97, 99.

14 Coox (1985), p.672.

15 Hata, Izawa and Shores (2002), pp.17–20; Millman (2010), p.31; Kotelnikov 2009, pp.46, 48, 50, 51, 52; Nedialkov; pp.73,74, 83, 85, 89, 88, 90, 92, 99.

Chapter 6

1 Erickson (2001), pp.532–533; Kolomiets; Lopez and Otkhmezuri, pp.245–246; Hill, p.99; Hooton (2013), pp.58–61.

2 Goldman (2012); pp.131–134; McDonald (2017), pp.262, 269–271; Coox (1985), p.667.

3 Coox (1985), p.676.

4 Japanese Studies on Manchuria vol. XI, Part 3, Book C, pp.375, 376, 380, 382–383, 599–300, 606–613; Erickson (2001), p.534; Schultz (2011), p.48; Lopez & Otkhmezru (2009), pp.246–248; Goldman (2012), pp.139–140; McDonald (2017), pp.272–273, 277–279; Hooton (2013), pp.62, 64; Hill pp.100–101; Coox (1985), pp.663–664, 667, 669, 674–677, 681.

5 Coox, p.713.

6 Coox p.732.

7 Japanese Studies on Manchuria vol. XI, Part 3, Book C, pp.376, 380, 382–383, 385, 389, 618–19; Hooton (2013), pp.64–65; Goldman (2012), pp.141–143, 145; McDonald (2017), pp.274–275, 280–283, 285, 287; Coox (1985), pp.708, 713–715, 718, 721, 725–726, 728–733.

8 Coox (1985), p.672.

9   Japanese Studies on Manchuria vol. XI, Part 3, Book B, pp.342, 344; Japanese Studies on Manchuria vol. XI, Part 3, Book C, p.381; Nedialkov pp.107–110, 112, 114, 115, 117, 119–233, 123–125, 129–130, 138, 141; Kotelnikov (2009) pp.61–63, 65, 67–68, 72–77–8; Coox (1985) pp.671–672, 685, 687; Hata, Izawa and Shores (2002), pp.21–23.

10 Japanese Studies on Manchuria vol. XI, Part 3, Book C, pp.390, 390, 400, 402 617, 620, 622; Goldman (2012), p.145–148; McDonald (2017) pp.288–291; Coox (1985), pp.738–739, 743, 757; Hooton (2013), p.65.

11 *Japanese Studies on Manchuria vol. XI, Part 3, Book C*, p.410.

12 Japanese Studies on Manchuria vol. XI, Part 3, Book C, pp.392–393, 399, 407–408, 412, 417, 433–434; Goldman (2012) pp.149–151; McDonald (2017), pp.291–293.

13 Japanese Studies on Manchuria vol. XI, Part 3, Book C, pp.460–461; McDonald (2017), p.295; Coox (1985), pp.914–916; Hooton (2013), p.67; Kolomiets.

ABOUT THE AUTHOR

Adrien Fontanellaz, from Switzerland, is a military history researcher and author. He developed a passion for military history at an early age and has progressively narrowed his studies to modern-day conflicts. He is a member of the Scientific Committee of the Pully-based *Centre d'Histoire et de Prospective Militaires* (Military History and Prospectives Centre), and regularly contributes for the *Revue Militaire Suisse* and various French military history magazines. This is his 14th title for Helion's @War series.